TWENTIETH
CENTURY
WORLD
HISTORY

JAPAN

IN THE TWENTIETH CENTURY

RICHARD TAMES

Batsford Academic and Educational Ltd *London*

CONTENTS

The Japanese	3
Japan Emerges	11
Search for Security	21
The Dark Valley	28
Total War 1941 - 1954	36
Occupation 1945 - 1952	47
Democracy - Japanese Style	54
The Economic Miracle	64
Japan Transformed?	72
The Silent Superpower	83
Date List	93
Books for Further Reading	94
Index	95

© Richard Tames 1981
First published 1981

Typeset by Tek-Art Ltd, London SE20
and printed in Great Britain by
R J Acford Ltd
Chichester, Sussex
for the publishers
Batsford Academic and Educational Ltd,
an imprint of B T Batsford Ltd,
4 Fitzhardinge Street, London W1H 0AH

ISBN 0 7134 3966 1

ACKNOWLEDGMENT

The Author and Publishers thank the following
for their kind permission to reproduce copyright
illustrations: International Society for Educational Information, Tokyo for figs 3, 9; Japan
Information Service for figs 1, 5, 34, 42, 49;
Jetro Photo Service for figs 2, 4, 32, 41, 43, 45,
46, 47, 48, 51; Mansell Collection Ltd for figs
10, 12, 13, 14, 15, 16, 17, 18, 19, 21, 22, 23,
24, 26, 28, 29. The maps were drawn by
Mr R. Britto. Other illustrations are the property
of the author.

THE JAPANESE

Japan is the sixth most populous country in the world, with a population in 1980 of 116 million. It is the world's second largest economy, with an annual gross national product twice as great as that of the United Kingdom. Japan is the world's largest producer of television sets and motor cars. Japan is also the world's largest importer of energy and the world's third largest democracy. Japan is, in other words, a very important country.

Yet knowledge of Japan in other countries, and especially in the West, is very limited. For Europeans, Japan is literally half a world away. Geographically remote, it is also culturally quite distinct. Like Britain, Japan is a constitutional monarchy whose prosperity relies on trade in manufactured goods with distant markets. Unlike Britain, Japan has a Shinto and Buddhist heritage, rather than a Christian one, and whereas Britain is a multi-racial society, Japan, apart from a small number of Koreans, has no ethnic minorities.

Perhaps the most striking difference between the two countries is the matter of language. Britain is part of an English-speaking world. Migration and the exchange of views and knowledge takes place easily, not only between Britain and North America, Australasia and the West Indies, where English is the dominant language, but also with Africa and South Asia, where it is the major language of the educated elite. But only the Japanese speak Japanese. It is a language quite distinctly different from Chinese, although it is written with an adapted form of Chinese script, and from the other major languages of the world. There are probably only a few thousand non-Japanese, perhaps only a few hundred, who could claim to have a real mastery of the language.

The Japanese do not, as a rule, emigrate, though there are small communities of Japanese descent in Peru, Brazil and Hawaii and along the western coast of North America. And few foreigners (about 60,000) live in Japan. Japanese rarely marry non-Japanese and only very recently have they begun to travel abroad in large numbers (about 3 million per year by the end of the 1970s, rather fewer than the number of British tourists going annually to Spain). These social factors, coupled with the problem of language, make it difficult for Japanese to get to know foreigners at first hand, or for foreigners to get to know them.

In these circumstances, it is, perhaps, not very surprising that so many misleading ideas about Japan are still current in different parts of the world. The Japanese do not, for example, work much longer hours than their British counterparts. Nor do they work for lower wages. And they do, from time to time, go on strike. They also play tennis, eat hamburgers, get drunk and watch a great deal of television.

All these statements about the Japanese are generalizations. They do not, of course, apply to each particular Japanese, and one can make some important qualifications about each of them. Some groups of workers (e.g. railwaymen) are much more likely to go on strike than others (computer operators). Japanese men are far more likely to get drunk than Japanese women, and so on. Nevertheless, we can make broad statements about the beliefs and behaviour of the Japanese people, and, in many cases, we can back

1   Mount Fuji and cherry blossom — the beauty of Nature supplies the traditional symbols of Japan.

these up with evidence from statistical records and opinion surveys. Japan is one of the very few Asian countries which produces comprehensive and accurate statistics. Interpreting them, however, takes skill and judgement and in this we are assisted by the many accounts of the Japanese people, at various points in their history, which have been written by visiting foreigners.

Some views expressed by foreign visitors have been made to look rather silly by the later course of events. Consider these judgements by English writers of the 1880s:

> The Japanese have a moderate future before them. They are a happy race, and being content with little are not likely to achieve much. (*The Japan Herald*, an English-language newspaper, produced for foreign residents)

> The army of Japan is quite good for Asia, but it could not stand up to European troops as its men lack the true military instinct. (Captain Grierson, British War Office observer)

> The Japanese should have no concern with business; the country ought to be put in a glass case, and paid to go on looking pretty. (Rudyard Kipling, poet and writer)

Many scholars are unhappy about the term "national character" and it certainly must be used with great care. Where a nation is newly formed, like Nigeria, or very large, like India, the characteristics of the people who make up that nation may be more strongly influenced by their past traditions or by present regional differences, than by a sense of common nationhood. But Japan is, perhaps, something of a special case. The Japanese have never been colonized or formed part of a larger empire. And they are the only nation in the world today consisting of more than 100 million people, all of whom speak the same language and are of the same ethnic stock. In other words, the Japanese actually feel very Japanese, and many books are written and published in Japan each year about Japanese society, the Japanese character, the country's prospects in the twenty-first century and similar subjects.

Impressions of the Japanese by non-Japanese writers go back to the third century AD, when Chinese visitors noted that they were extremely brave, strictly governed and avoided the display of strong emotions such as grief or jealousy. The observations of later writers have tended to repeat

4

and confirm these and other traits as characteristic features, that are long-term continuities in Japanese behaviour and the values that mould it:

The Japanese are very ambitious of honours and distinctions and think themselves superior to all nations in military glory and valour. They prize and honour all that has to do with war . . . [and] . . . value arms more than any people I have ever seen.

They are very polite to each other, but not to foreigners whom they utterly despise. (St Francis Xavier, 1552)

The people of this island of Japan are good of nature, courteous above measure and valiant

2   A wedding in Japan — costume and ritual stress the importance of tradition on such occasions.

in war (Will Adams, c. 1610)

Bold . . . heroic . . . revengeful . . . desirous of fame . . . very industrious and inured to hardships . . . great lovers of civility and good manners, and very nice in keeping themselves, their clothes and houses, clean and neat . . . (Engelbert Kaempfer, c. 1690)

The average judgement formed by those who have lived some time among the Japanese seems to resolve itself into three principal items on the credit side, which are cleanliness, kindliness and a refined artistic taste, and three items on the debit side, namely vanity, unbusinesslike habits and an incapacity for appreciating abstract ideas.

The travelled Japanese consider our three most prominent characteristics to be dirt, laziness and superstition. (Basil Hall Chamberlain, 1904)

If there is any single characteristic which over the last century has been remarked upon as being most distinctive to the Japanese and of most central importance in understanding their society, it is what one might call "groupishness". In any society people have to learn to get along with one another, a process which involves learning to live within generally accepted ideas of good manners and proper behaviour. What is perhaps unusual about Japan, as contrasted with Western countries, is the extent to which ideals and customs are related to the needs and harmony of the group to which people belong, rather than to the desires and impulses of the individual. In the family, at school and at work, Japanese are not encouraged to "do their own thing"; the underlying notion is rather that expressed in a traditional proverb — "the nail that sticks up gets knocked down". This may seem very repressive, but it must be remembered that the emphasis on group harmony is not enforced by political or legal coercion (though in the feudal past the laws were intended to keep people firmly "in their place", as they were in

3   Planting out rice seedlings — a practical demonstration of the philosophy of teamwork.

4   Work together, eat together — workmates are also friends.

feudal Europe). Post-war Japan has no censorship. Critics of the government are not locked up. Demonstrators are free to demonstrate.

The stress on group harmony is more a matter of positive encouragements than of negative sanctions. People who work together also take their leisure together. Office colleagues regularly go drinking one or two nights a week. Employees of large firms go on holiday to company-owned hotels. Farmer's wives from the same village will organize tours to beauty-spots and historic sites. At work, employees like their boss to take an interest in their personal lives and they will often invite him to family occasions such as weddings and parties. Political factions and university departments often have the same family-like atmosphere, with the leader or professor playing the role of "parent" to the members of the group, by helping them win promotion or settling their disputes. In return, they owe him their loyalty and support.

Many theories have been advanced to explain the Japanese emphasis on the needs of the group. Some scholars have emphasized the historical

5   Shinjuku — the newest face of Tokyo.

6   The past preserved — Kyomizudera temple, Kyoto.

significance of Japan's "rice-culture". For two thousand years the Japanese have had to co-operate in the agricultural tasks of ground-clearing and terracing, planting, irrigating and harvesting rice, and this has led to a wider sense of working together for the good of the community. But if this explanation is right, why is the group emphasis not equally strong throughout the rice lands of East and South-East Asia? And how has it survived in Japan into the age of industrialization? Other scholars have pointed out how the Japanese have always been vulnerable to natural disasters such as earthquakes, volcanoes, floods and typhoons. These hazards have forced the Japanese to cultivate a talent for survival and reconstruction, a talent further reinforced by a history which has been marked by periods of anarchy and civil war.

Another school of thought emphasizes the closeness of the relationship which has existed for centuries between the rulers and the ruled. In the early seventeenth century William Adams, the first Englishman to live in Japan, remarked that the people were "veri subject to thear gouvernours and superiores". Under the Tokugawa dynasty (1603-1868), public order and stability was the government's main objective, and under the Meiji leaders (1868-1912), conscription and mass education were used to make the people into loyal and hard-working subjects of the emperor.

Whatever the origins of Japanese "groupishness", its importance must never be overlooked. Writing in 1943, John Morris, an English teacher employed by the Japanese government from 1938-42, warned that:

The Germans cracked in 1918 and there is every reason for supposing that in due course they will crack again. But the psychology of the Japanese people is different, and I believe they will never give in; they will go on lowering their standard of living, if necessary until the daily ration is barely sufficient to support life, but the people will not crack . . . any talk of a Japanese collapse is merely a dangerous form of wishful thinking.

Under a militaristic government, the national loyalty of the Japanese was mobilized to serve the needs of war. Since 1945 the Japanese have mobilized themselves for the task of economic reconstruction. At the same time, they have managed to combine rapidly rising standards of living, health and education with a low level of crime and domestic violence. Japan, so often accused of imitation, perhaps deserves to be imitated in return.

YOUNG HISTORIAN

A

1 In what ways, if any , is Japan unique?
2 Summarize the main differences between Japan and Britain.
3 In what ways are the Japanese "groupish"?
4 Explain the meaning of (a) ethnic minorities, (b) elite, (c) repressive, (d) coercion, (e) censorship, (f) sanctions, (g) factions, (h) anarchy, (i) militaristic.

B

What advice would you give to a Westerner wanting to go to live in Japan for a while?

C

Draw up a month-long itinerary for a tour of Japan. Make sure that it covers different areas. What sorts of people would it be most helpful to meet? Make up three questions which you think it would be most helpful to ask *every* Japanese you would meet.

D

Draw a map of Japan and mark in the major cities and mountainous areas.

JAPAN EMERGES

JAPAN AND THE WEST

Throughout history the Japanese have absorbed influences from the outside world and made them part of their own way of life. In the sixth and seventh centuries AD Japan learned much from the more advanced civilization of China, then ruled by the brilliant T'ang dynasty. Buddhism, the Chinese system of writing and Chinese methods of government and town planning were among the many innovations which were then adopted by the Japanese. But Japan never became a mere imitator of China, or lost its distinctive character, whether in the arts or in politics or in such details of daily life as dress and diet. As we shall see, this same openness to foreign ideas, coupled with a concern and an ability to preserve Japan's particular identity, was later to characterize the country's relations with the West.

Europeans first came to Japan in 1543. As the country was in the throes of civil war, no authority existed to control the spread of Western ideas and goods — chiefly in the form of Christianity and guns. By the 1580s some half a million Japanese had converted to the new religion. By the 1630s, however, a new dynasty, the Tokugawa, had established themselves in power. Fearing that the Westerners might upset the peace which they had so painfully imposed on Japan, they forbade the practice of Christianity and expelled all Westerners except the Dutch, who were confined to an island in Nagasaki harbour. Japanese were forbidden to travel abroad, on pain of death,

and the building of ocean-going ships was banned.

This "closed country" policy was kept up for two centuries — during which the Western world was transformed by the spread of democratic ideas and the beginnings of industrialization. The ordinary people of Japan knew nothing of these events; but their rulers learned from the Dutch merchants how much the world was changing. A few scholars wanted to learn more about the West and especially about its progress in science and medicine. But most of those who gave any thought to the matter simply wanted Japan to be able to maintain its isolation.

As a result of its war against Mexico in 1846-48, the United States acquired California and thus became a Pacific power. It now saw China, where Britain, France and other Western nations were trading busily, as a region of great commercial promise and Japan, it was decided, would be an extremely convenient source of supply for American ships seeking coal and provisions. It seemed to the Americans extremely unreasonable that Japan should shut itself off from peaceful trade with other nations. In 1853, therefore, a squadron of the US Navy, under the command of Commodore Matthew Perry, was sent to Japan to demand that its ports be opened to trade.

The Tokugawa, knowing that they were powerless to resist steam-powered iron warships, were compelled to sign a series of what became known as "unequal treaties", first of all with the USA and then with the other Western powers. These treaties opened up a number of Japanese ports to trade, prohibited Japan from imposing any but very low tariffs on imports from the West and, most humiliating of all, granted foreigners living in Japan "extra-territorial status". This meant that, if they committed a crime, they would be tried in a consular court under the laws of their own country. To the Japanese, this was as much as saying that Japan was not a civilized country and that its laws need not therefore be respected by non-Japanese.

The weakness of the Tokugawa in the face of Western demands undermined their authority to rule. For seven centuries Japan had been governed by a shogun (literally a "barbarian-subduing generalissimo"), a military dictator who ruled on behalf of the emperor and in his name. Now the Tokugawa shogun had been shown to be powerless. An anti-Tokugawa coalition formed, based on the Satsuma and Choshu clans, under the slogan "Revere the Emperor and expel the barbarian". In 1868, after a brief civil war, they overthrew the Toku-

gawa and took power in the name of the young emperor Meiji.

Once in power, however, the leaders of this "Meiji Restoration" came to appreciate the weakness of the Japanese position against the West. Seeing that it was impossible to repudiate the "unequal treaties" and "expel the barbarian", they determined to "Westernize" Japan as the only way to prevent it from becoming an outright colony. Their new slogan was *"fukoku kyohei"* — "enrich the country, strengthen the army".

7   Southern barbarians — Portuguese traders to Japan are depicted on this sixteenth-century gilded screen. Notice how the Japanese artist has elongated the legs of the figures to accentuate their height.

8   Founder of the dynasty — Tokugawa Ieyasu (1542-1616).

13

As Foreign Minister Inoue put it in 1887

What we have to do is to transform our empire and our people and make the empire like the countries of Europe and our people like the people of Europe. To put it differently we have to establish a new, European-style empire on the edge of Asia.

THE WESTERNIZATION OF JAPAN

Japan's transformation into a modern industrial state was accomplished with astonishing rapidity. By the 1890s motor cars and motion pictures were seen in Tokyo within months of their first appearance in London and Paris. How can this remarkable series of changes be accounted for?

Japan's situation on the eve of its modernization was unlike that of most developing nations today. Its people were undivided by race, language or religion. Centuries of stern Tokugawa rule had accustomed them to obey their government and to work diligently. Literacy was widespread, as was respect for learning. The Tokugawa had also bequeathed to their successors a priceless asset — a competent and uncorrupt civil service. The Meiji modernizers could therefore give orders, confident that they would be obeyed, and levy taxes, confident that they would be collected. Geography, too, seemed to favour Japan. An island nation, it had no tense border areas, but enjoyed the advantage of good communications by coastal shipping and a temperate climate which spared it the ravages of tropical disease. International trends were also favourable. The perfection of steam-ships and bulk-freight carriers in the 1870s boosted a general expansion in world trade, and Japan benefited from a rapid growth in the demand for raw silk. This brought in the foreign exchange needed to pay for the advanced technology which Japan was obliged to import from the West.

During the first decade of modernization the government worked to establish a suitable environment for economic growth, and a uniform currency as well as standard weights and measures were imposed throughout the country. Universal

9 "Old Bruin" — Commodore Matthew C. Perry.

elementary education was introduced, a postal and telegraph service created, and a programme of railway building and road improvement begun. "Model factories" were set up and large numbers of foreign, mostly British, experts were brought in to teach new technological skills. Agricultural improvement and research were encouraged and the Northern island of Hokkaido was opened up for settlement and cultivation.

14

These policies were not implemented without opposition. Resistance among the ordinary people could be, and was, crushed by the police. But disagreements also broke out among the ruling elite. Some thought that the Westernization policy threatened to destroy the unique character of Japan's way of life. Others wanted to assert Japan's power by conquering Korea and staking out a pre-eminent position for Japan in East Asia. These opposition elements rose in rebellion in 1877, but were defeated by the government's new, Western-trained army, an army no longer of samurai but of peasant conscripts. Their victory symbolized the dominance of the modernizers in guiding the affairs of the nation.

In the countryside, the life-style of the ordinary people was relatively little altered. The diet and dress and homes of the peasants were not very different from what their grandparents had known. Most consumer goods, such as furnishings or household utensils, were still made by craftsmen, using hand-tools or simple machines. But even here life was changing. All children went to school, where they were taught to be loyal and obedient subjects of the emperor. Teenage sons went away to serve in the army. Teenage daughters went away to work in textile mills. They knew what their grandparents had not known — that Japan was part of a wider world, a world that was changing and, in some ways, very threatening.

In the cities, Westernization was much more in evidence. Government officials wore European-style dress. Horse-drawn carriages took the place of palanquins. Young men, whose fathers had worn the two swords of a samurai, now earnestly discussed novel Western ideas, such as parliamentary government and women's rights, conscious that they were living in the glorious age of *"bummei-kaika"* — "civilization and enlightenment". Japanese children sang a song about "ten things worthy of imitation" — gas lamps, steam engines, horse carriages, cameras, telegrams, newspapers, schools, letter-post, steam-boats and lightning conductors.

It is important to emphasize that Japan's modernization was not a matter of mere "copying". The West offered differing models of advanced institutions and the Japanese were well able to choose carefully between them. Their army was trained by German advisers, their navy by British instructors. Their system of local government was based on the French one, while Americans were allotted a leading role in the development of Japanese agriculture and education. The Japanese government, moreover, took great care to avoid becoming dependent on foreigners. Only two loans were raised abroad; the rest of the capital for the development of industry and the re-equipping of the armed forces was raised from taxes. Foreign experts were carefully chosen, paid well, and sent home after they had trained Japanese to fill their posts.

Nowhere is the prudence of the Meiji modernizers more evident than in the matter of government itself. Naturally, the promotion of widespread economic and social changes and the introduction of Western political ideas encouraged discussion about the most appropriate form of government for Japan. During the 1880s opponents of the regime launched a movement for "people's rights", hoping that, if a parliament were to be established, they could use it to criticize the men around the emperor. Partly to head off this challenge, and partly to reinforce Japan's claim to have become a "modern" nation, the Meiji elite advised the emperor to grant a constitution.

This constitution was, after careful study and comparison, based on the constitution of the new German empire. Although an elected two-chamber Diet (parliament) was established, only a tiny proportion of the population was enfranchised and the Diet was given few powers. The emperor (and, therefore, in practice, his closest advisers) remained in personal command of the armed services (whose leaders had special access to him), retained the power to make war and peace, chose the members of the upper house of the Diet, and could dissolve the lower house of the Diet at will.

FOREIGN RELATIONS AFTER WESTERNIZATION

Japan's modernization was essentially a response to external pressures. By the 1890s the country

JOHN STANDS ALOOF.

RUSSIA. "IS HE TO HAVE ALL *THIS?*"
JOHN BULL. "WELL—HE'S PLAYED A SQUARE GAME—*I* DON'T SEE ANY CALL TO INTERFERE!"

SWAIN sc

was in a position to begin asserting itself in international affairs. The Ryukyus, the Bonin Islands and Okinawa, possible bases for invasion, had already been annexed. Concern focused on Korea — "a dagger pointed at the heart of Japan", as a foreign military adviser had put it. Both Japan and China had extensive trading interests in this peninsula which was ruled by a conservative dynasty, resistant to the possibilities of reform and modernization. Both China and Japan intrigued in Korean court politics, each hoping to steal an advantage over the other.

In 1894 an internal uprising in Korea led both powers to send in troops, and the eventual outcome was a war from which Japan emerged victorious within a year. The scale and speed of China's defeat by Japan was evidence of this country's new-found power. Peace terms were

10 Triple Intervention — Russia, France and Germany "advised" Japan not to accept control of the Liaotung Peninsula from China. Britain (represented in this *Punch* cartoon by John Bull) was not yet allied to Japan, but was sympathetic to its cause.

agreed in the Treaty of Shimonoseki; Korean independence was recognized (i.e. China gave up its claim to regard Korea as a vassal state); Japan was ceded Formosa (Taiwan), the Pescadores and the Liaotung peninsula. China also agreed to pay Japan a sizeable indemnity, to open four new treaty ports and to negotiate a new treaty of commerce.

The Japanese public was well pleased with these terms. But this pleasure did not last. Within a week Russia, France and Germany "advised" Japan not to accept control of the Liaotung

16

peninsula. Faced with this "Triple Intervention", Japan, having no allies, was forced to swallow its pride and, following the emperor's call to "bear the unbearable", submit.

The exposure of China's weakness increased the desire of the Western powers to entrench themselves even more securely in Chinese territories by means of commercial, legal and military privileges. Japan could scarcely regard these developments with indifference, and, in particular, feared the growing power of Russia, whose railway-building programme seemed designed to secure a dominant position in China's northern regions.

At the same time, Japan's international standing rose rapidly as a result of the unexpectedly swift victory over China. Even before the war, Britain had agreed to revise the "unequal treaties" and give up its extra-territorial rights. The Japanese minister in London noted with pride that this new agreement enabled Japan to "avoid the insults suffered over the past 30 years and, at one go, enter the 'Fellowship of Nations'. Truly a matter for great congratulation". Other powers followed suit.

When the anti-foreign "Boxer" rising broke out in North China in 1900, Japan acted with the Western powers to rescue the diplomats be-sieged in Peking and to uphold foreign treaty rights. Japanese troops made up almost half of the 20,000-strong relief expedition and greatly impressed their Western allies by their courage and discipline.

In 1902 Japan's new status was dramatically affirmed by the signature of a treaty of alliance with Great Britain — the first military pact on equal terms between a Western and a non-Western nation in modern times. The British, challenged in home waters by the growing naval power of Germany, and hoping to secure their position along the Yangtze in central China, recognized the value of Japanese naval co-operation. The Japanese, fearing a repetition of the Triple Intervention, were anxious to have the support of a strong ally in the event of a future confrontation with a Western power. The alliance recognized Japan's interest in Korea, "in a peculiar degree politically as well as commercially and industrially". Both nations pledged themselves to neutrality if either engaged in war with a third power, but each agreed to aid the other if it were attacked by two or more powers. In effect, this meant that Japan could settle its differences with Russia without fear of having

11   Scene of the Russo-Japanese War 1904-5.

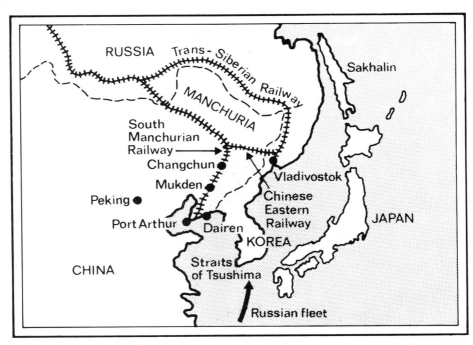

17

to take on France, Russia's ally, as well.

Russia had, in 1896, gained a concession from Peking to build a "Chinese Eastern Railway" across Manchuria to the naval base of Vladivostok ("Ruler of the East"). This greatly shortened the original route of the Trans-Siberian Railway, which had been begun in 1891 to link European Russia with its Pacific provinces. In 1898 Russia secured a lease of the Liaotung peninsula and, with it, the right to build a "South Manchurian Railway" to join the Chinese Eastern Railway to the ports of the peninsula, Dairen and Port Arthur. These railway concessions enabled Russia to undertake a full military occupation of Manchuria during the "Boxer" crisis. Negotiations between Japan and Russia failed to reach a compromise over spheres of influence. On 6 February 1904 Japan broke off relations and on 8 February launched a night torpedo attack on the Russian fleet in Port Arthur. A formal declaration of war followed two days later.

In May 1904 Japanese forces crossed the Yalu river from Korea into Manchuria, while sea-borne forces seized Dairen and besieged Port Arthur, which finally fell in January 1905. In March, after a long and bloody battle, the Japanese took Mukden, the chief city of Manchuria. The Russians placed their last hope on their Baltic fleet, a hastily assembled armada of forty-five ships, which took nine months to sail more than half way round the world and was annihilated by the Japanese navy in the Straits of Tsushima on 27 May 1905.

Japan's superiority over mighty Russia seemed complete, but the strain of war had brought the Japanese economy very near collapse, and both sides were grateful to accept US President Theodore Roosevelt's offer to initiate peace negotiations. The Treaty of Portsmouth, signed on 5 September 1905, recognized Japan's "paramount interest in Korea", and assigned to Japan both the Russian lease on the Liaotung peninsula and the South Manchurian Railway as far north as Changchun. In addition, Russia ceded the southern half of the island of Sakhalin with its valuable timber and fishing grounds. While the Tsar's government battled to suppress revolution at home, Japan's position in North-East Asia seemed secure at last. Free of all foreign competitors in Korea, Japan made it first of all a protectorate and then, in 1910, an outright colony. Russia, now preoccupied with internal reform and events in Europe, agreed to co-operate

In action — 12 (below) Japanese naval gunners and 13 (right) infantry, 1904-5.

with Japan in defending the two countries' respective interests in East Asia.

JAPAN IN 1912

By the time of the death of emperor Meiji in 1912, therefore, Japan had achieved the parity with the Western powers which Japanese statesmen had sought with such determination for half a century. Throughout Asia, nationalists, bitterly resentful of colonial rule, thrilled at Japan's destruction of the myth of Western invincibility. That Japan had become an imperialist power was less freely acknowledged.

YOUNG HISTORIAN

A

1 Why has Japan been so influenced by China?
2 Why did Japan "Westernize" after 1868? In what ways did Japan *not* "Westernize"?
3 In what ways was Japan more powerful in 1912 than it had been in 1868?
4 Are there any lessons that the developing countries of today can learn from Japan's experience in the late nineteenth century?
5 Explain the meaning of (a) extra-territorial status, (b) shogun, (c) dynasty, (d) indemnity, (e) protectorate, (f) samurai.

B

1 Write a conversation between two samurai, in which one argues in favour of learning from the West and the other in favour of maintaining the policy of a "closed country".

2 Imagine you are a young Japanese who has come to study in England in the 1870s. Write a letter to your parents, describing the things that have most surprised and interested you.

C

1 Write a series of newspaper headlines covering the main events in Japanese history from 1868 to 1912.
2 Imagine you are an old man in Japan around 1910. Write a letter to your grandson, describing the changes you have seen in your lifetime.

D

1 Draw a map to show the expansion of Japanese territory between 1868 and 1910.
2 Draw a series of diagrams showing the growth in Japan's industry during this period.

SEARCH FOR SECURITY

A NEW EMPEROR

Historians have called the generation after the death of emperor Meiji in 1912 the period of "Taisho democracy". Taisho ("Great Righteousness") refers to the reign-name of the new emperor. Democracy refers to two tendencies which were characteristic of these years — (1) the struggle by the Diet and the party politicians to exert more influence over national policy-making, at the expense of the high-ranking officers and advisers who surrounded the emperor, and (2) the movement on the part of the intellectuals and working people to agitate for wider popular participation in the nation's political life.

The Taisho era was one of progress, confusion and uncertainty. Rapid industrial expansion was accompanied by growing tensions between rich and poor. New styles of living and radical political ideas led conservative Japanese to fear the power of "dangerous thoughts". In foreign affairs Japan achieved the acknowledged status of a first-rank power, yet seemed unable to establish stable economic and strategic arrangements with other nations.

THE FIRST WORLD WAR

When war broke out in Europe in 1914, Japan, as Britain's ally, attacked the German possessions in Shantung. Britain was not eager for Japanese assistance, but Japanese policy-makers saw the opportunity to strengthen Japan's position in northern China and the Pacific, while the Western powers were distracted by war. China, torn apart by revolution and war-lord rule, was powerless to prevent a rapid Japanese take-over of the Shantung peninsula, with its modernized port of Tsingtao, its railways and its coal-mines. Encouraged by this success, the Japanese government in 1915 secretly presented to China a list of "Twenty One Demands", grouped in five categories:

Group One — confirmed Japan's rights in Shantung and over the future disposal of the province.

Group Two — demanded that the 25-year leases on Port Arthur, Dairen and the South Manchurian Railroad which Japan had been granted in 1905 be extended to 99 years, and that the economic privileges of Japanese in Eastern Mongolia and South Manchuria be improved still further.

Group Three — aimed to promote the iron and coal industries in the Yangtze valley, under Japanese control.

Group Four — pledged China not to assign its coastal territories to other powers.

Group Five (which the Japanese called "desires", rather than "demands") — required the Chinese to take on teams of Japanese advisers in their government, police and armed forces, to allow Japanese to own land in the interior and to build more railways. If accepted, these Group Five conditions would virtually have reduced China to the status of a Japanese colony.

The Chinese government leaked news of the Japanese ultimatum and played for time. The reaction of the Western powers, and especially of America, was one of hostility to Japan, and, accordingly, Japan settled for Chinese acceptance of most of the demands in the first four groups. By the threat of force, Japan thus strengthened its economic grip on the mainland of East Asia. But the price it paid for this advantage was to have outraged Chinese national feeling and to have aroused among the Western powers a lasting suspicion of Japan's ultimate objectives in its dealings with its neighbours.

In 1917, however, the hard-pressed Allies, in return for much-needed Japanese naval support, agreed in a series of secret treaties between Japan, Britain, France, Italy and Russia that they would support Japanese claims to German territories in China and the Pacific at the post-war peace conference.

Japan attended the Paris peace negotiations with three major aims in view — to secure control of the former German islands in the Pacific, which it had occupied since the beginning of the war (the Marianas, Carolines and Marshalls); to be confirmed in its possession of Shantung; and to insert in the covenant of the proposed League of Nations a declaration of racial equality. None of these aims was entirely achieved. The German Pacific islands were acquired, not as outright colonies, but as mandates, for whose good government Japan was answerable, in theory, to the League of Nations. With regard to Shantung, Japan was forced by Chinese and American opposition to negotiate its position, despite the support of the other Allies for its claims. And the racial equality clause was rejected, thanks largely to pressure from Australia, which feared that such a clause might challenge its policy of prohibiting non-white immigration.

Japan, although one of the "Big Five", could regard the post-war settlement with little satisfaction, despite having significantly improved its strategic and economic position at no great military cost. While Britain and France had carved up the remnants of the Ottoman Empire and awarded each other Germany's former colonies in Africa, and while America's President Wilson preached his message of international good-will, Japan had been obliged to compromise what it

regarded as its own legitimate interests, and to suffer, in the matter of the racial equality clause, a wounding rebuff to Japanese pride.

THE JAPANESE IN SIBERIA

At the Paris Peace Conference one of the principal combatants of the Great War was notable by its absence — Russia, or, as it had now become, the Soviet Union. In March 1918 the new Bolshevik government had concluded a separate peace with Germany, by the Treaty of Brest-Litovsk, to enable it to withdraw from the war and concentrate on imposing its authority at home. The position in Siberia was particularly critical, for here the Bolshevik armies faced not only free-lance bandits and would-be war-lords but also the more formidable opposition of anti-revolutionary "White Russian" forces under Admiral Kolchak, who had established a government at Omsk. The situation was further complicated by the presence of a well-organized army of former Czech prisoners-of-war which had been intended to cross Russia from west to east so that they might eventually join the Allies in France. When, after Brest-Litovsk, the Bolsheviks, now at peace with Germany, tried to disarm the Czechs, they resisted. And the Allies responded to this resistance by mounting an expeditionary force to "rescue" the Czechs. Armed intervention, on whatever pretext, obviously gave the Allies political leverage in a confused situation and opened up the possibility of establishing some sort of control over Siberia or at least of denying such control to the Bolsheviks. These ambitions seem to have been most prominent in the thinking of the Japanese military, for while the British and French sent only token contingents and the United States less than 10,000 troops, the Japanese despatched some 70,000.

However, Japan's armed intervention in Siberia was to prove a painful and expensive failure. The White Russian government collapsed by the end of 1919 and, as the war in Europe had long since ended, the "rescue" of the Czechs had become rather an irrelevant issue to everyone but themselves. Nevertheless, when the Western powers withdrew their forces, Japanese troops continued to occupy the area between Vladivostok and Chita and in 1920 took over Northern Sakhalin as a reprisal for the massacre of some Japanese soldiers by Russian partisans. Allied pressure and the unpopularity of the expedition in Japan eventually led to the withdrawal of Japanese forces from the Russian mainland in 1922 and in 1925 from Northern Sakhalin, where Japan was granted fishing and mining rights. These were Japan's only gains from the whole costly episode. Indeed, the net effect was largely to confirm Western fears of Japanese expansionism and thus to aggravate still further the delicate problem of securing a durable post-war settlement in East Asia and the Pacific. Such a settlement was the main objective of the nine-power conference which convened in Washington in November 1921.

THE WASHINGTON CONFERENCE

The complex negotiations of the Washington conference resulted in a series of treaties settling the inter-related problems of great power alliances, naval armaments and the status of China. The main features of these agreements were as follows:

The Four Power Treaty (13 December 1921)
(a) The signatories (USA, Britain, Japan and France) agreed to respect each other's Pacific island possessions.
(b) The signatories agreed to consult in the event of a dispute over the treaty or a threat to their Pacific possessions from another power.
(c) The treaty was to last for ten years.

This treaty superseded the Anglo-Japanese alliance which both Britain and Japan had some interest in extending but which America and the Commonwealth states disliked. Its major weakness was that it was largely a statement of the goodwill of the parties concerned and embodied no procedure by which a serious threat to the peace of the Pacific could be dealt with.

The Five Power Treaty (5 February 1922)
(a) The signatories (USA, Britain, Japan, France and Italy) accepted that the capital ships (battleships, large cruisers and aircraft-carriers) of their navies should be limited in the following ratio – US and Britain 5; Japan 3; France and Italy 1.75, with a maximum tonnage for the US and Britain of 520,000. (For the first three powers, this involved considerable scrapping of ships in commission and under construction.)
(b) No new capital ships were to be built for ten years.
(c) No new naval bases were to be built in the Pacific (defined to include Hong Kong but not Singapore, Alaska, Hawaii or the offshore islands of Canada and Australia).
(d) The treaty was to remain in effect until December 1936 and could be terminated thereafter at two years' notice, by any signatory.

The Five Power Treaty headed off the danger and expense of a naval arms race and gave Japan a local supremacy in the Western Pacific, in return for accepting an inferior capital ship ratio overall.

The Nine Power Treaty (6 February 1922)
The signatory powers (the US, Britain, France, Japan, Italy, Belgium, the Netherlands, Portugal and China) agreed:
(a) to respect the sovereignty, independence, neutrality and territorial integrity of China;
(b) to assist in its economic development and in the establishment of a stable and effective government;
(c) to uphold the principle of equal opportunity for the commerce and industry of all nations in China;
(d) to abstain from infringing the established rights and security of friendly states in respect of their territories and interests in China.

In effect, this treaty made the favoured American principle of an "Open Door" for the commerce of all nations part of an international agreement for the first time. It attempted to halt the further dismemberment of China, but recognized existing unequal-treaty rights. Like the Four Power Treaty, it lacked an enforcement proce-

14 Popular rights — women factory workers protest against low wages, 1920s.

dure, for signatories had no obligation to aid China against a violator of the terms.

China itself gained little from the Washington conference beyond some concessions on tariffs and a promise (eventually fruitless) to examine the issue of extra-territoriality. But Britain and the US did pressure Japan into returning Kiaochow to China, though it retained control of the Tsinan-Tsingtao railway for a further fifteen years, while the Chinese bought it back by stages.

The Washington agreements reduced tension in East Asia, improved relations between the US and Japan, and gave China something of a breathing-space in which to re-organize its affairs. These achievements were worthwhile, but rested on no very secure foundation. Should any of the major powers involved in the region see its vital interests threatened, the agreements in themselves contained no obvious means by which the use of force could be prevented.

EFFECTS OF THE FIRST WORLD WAR IN JAPAN

The Great War produced for Japan domestically

the same mixture of advantages and difficulties as it produced internationally. Orders for war material from the Allies, coupled with the inability of Western nations to maintain their exports to Asia during wartime, gave the Japanese economy a massive boost. Heavy industry grew rapidly and Japanese traders secured a firm foothold in the markets of China and South-East Asia. In 1914 Japan had been a debtor nation, importing more each year than it exported; by 1919 the position was reversed, for the first time in Japanese history.

But, for the rapidly growing industrial working class of the towns, Japan's new economic strength appeared to bring few benefits. Working hours remained long, wages low, living conditions poor and the threat of unemployment never far away. These problems also applied to a sizeable proportion of the lower middle class of white-collar workers, such as clerks, shopkeepers and civil servants, although they were probably less inclined to listen to the arguments of trade unionists and Communist organizers, who were regarded with intense hostility by the government and the wealthy. In the countryside the situation was also difficult, with high rents a direct consequence of the pressure of Japan's swiftly-growing population (56 million in 1920, 64.5 million in 1930) on its limited area of cultivable land.

Dramatic evidence of widespread discontent was provided by the great "rice riots" of August 1918. The price of rice trebled between 1914 and 1918, partly because imports were not easily available and because the growth of industry had attracted labour away from farming, partly because some rice dealers were deliberately hoarding it to force up the price. When fishermen's wives in Toyama Prefecture rioted and forced a ten-per-cent price cut, their example was followed in more than 350 towns and villages. Nearly 100,000 troops were mobilized to restore order. The memory of these events was to haunt the Japanese establishment throughout the coming years. But their immediate result was to lead to the resignation of the entire cabinet and its replacement by a government under the leadership of Hara Takashi, the head of the Seiyukai, the largest political party in the Diet. This was a most important political development.

Until that time prime ministers had been chosen on the advice of the *genro*, the elder statesmen and generals who had master-minded the modernization of Japan. They had chosen men on the grounds of their loyalty and views; the political support they enjoyed in the Diet had not been regarded as important. Now it was. And this continued to be the case for the rest of the decade.

TOWARDS DEMOCRACY?

Foreign observers increasingly took the view that Japan was moving towards Western-style democracy. In 1925 all men over twenty-five were given the vote, the powers of the upper house were limited and the army was cut back from twenty-one divisions to seventeen. But in the same year a new "Peace Preservation Law" confirmed police powers to harass left-wingers. At the same time, repeated revelations of bribery and corruption among Diet members did little to improve their standing in the eyes of the public. Many critics saw politicians as greedy opportunists, concerned only to line their own pockets by promoting the interests of big business, which supplied the funds for their election expenses. The development of democratic politics was further weakened by the fact that, behind the scenes, service officers, bureaucrats and courtiers still exercised a great deal of influence. This partly hidden elite was more or less united in its hostility to mass-participation in politics and attacks on the rights of property. But personal ambitions and genuine differences of opinion also led to much factional in-fighting, both between and within the court, the armed services and the various ministries. The result of these rivalries was to confuse the process of decision-making and to lead to hesitant and uncertain leadership.

In these circumstances, it is not surprising that some thinkers began to call for drastic changes in Japanese politics, to solve the nation's problems. Communist and anarchist views were fashionable among some intellectuals and attracted the support of a minority of organized workers. But the views of the right-wing nationalists were more influential, especially among students

15 Acquiring an international outlook — young Japanese studying in Germany, 1920s.

and young army officers, many of whom came from farming families living on the edge of poverty. Among the various demands of the radical nationalists were: an end to the rule of corrupt party politicians; the rejection of Western fashions and ideas; a limit on the size of private fortunes; more help for the farmer; and an aggressive foreign policy. Such measures would constitute a "Showa Restoration", ("*Showa*" — "Enlightenment and Harmony" — was the reign-name chosen for the new emperor, Hirohito, in 1926), which would bring justice and prosperity at home and strengthen Japan's power abroad. Just how it was to be brought about was usually left rather

26

vague, apart from the fact that it was to be done in the name of the emperor and as an expression of his "real" wishes. However, it was quite clear that those who were seen as the main supporters and beneficiaries of the present system — Diet-members, industrialists and liberal intellectuals — were targets for attack and that attacks might not merely be verbal but also physical — and even fatal.

FOREIGN POLICY IN THE 1920s

Nothing disgusted right-wingers more than the conduct of Japan's foreign policy during the 1920s. Under Baron Shidehara (foreign minister 1924-27 and 1929-31), Japan's attitude to foreign problems was conciliatory. When, in 1924, the United States passed an "Oriental Exclusion Act", which deliberately discriminated against Japanese immigrants and was in violation of a previous agreement, Japan took no action beyond protest. When Japanese in China were attacked, the government seemed less willing than Britain was, in similar circumstances, to use force. When officers of the Kwantung Army stationed in Manchuria arranged the assassination of the local warlord, Chang Tso-lin, the government refused to take further advantage of the situation. And in 1930 the Japanese navy's plans to expand the fleet were overridden by the Hamaguchi government's willingness to sign the London Naval Treaty, which extended the agreements made in 1922. Hamaguchi was shot by a young right-wing fanatic in protest against this agreement. It was an ominous beginning to a decade already over-shadowed by the clouds of a world depression.

YOUNG HISTORIAN

A

1   In what senses was Japan a democracy between 1912 and 1931?
2   Why did Japanese relations with China get worse between 1914 and 1931?
3   Find out about the great Kanto earthquake of 1923.
4   Explain the meaning of (a) radical, (b) warlord, (c) ultimatum, (d) covenant, (e) mandates, (f) reprisal, (g) disbursements, (h) opportunists, (i) bureaucrats, (j) conciliatory, (k) fanatic.

B

Write a conversation between a liberal professor and an army officer in which they discuss their views of Japan's problems and what should be done about them.

C

Write a series of newspaper headlines outlining the main events of these years.

D

Write a series of slogans setting out some of the main ideas of the radical nationalists.

THE DARK VALLEY

THE DEPRESSION

The catastrophic decline in world trade which followed the great American stock-market crash of 1929 intensified Japan's economic and social problems. Particularly hard hit were the poorer farmers who relied on silk as a cash-crop. Silk exports dropped by two thirds, and Japan's export trade generally suffered from the effects of new tariff barriers as nations tried to fend off unemployment by keeping out foreign-

16 Saviours of the nation? — troops of the First Division leave Tokyo for duty in Manchuria.

17 Flags for freedom? — patriotic women sew the emblem of Japan's liberating mission in Asia. The flags were sent to Japanese men at the Front.

made goods. Each year the population increased by one million, and 400,000 new workers went in search of employment. Emigration offered no prospect of relief, because of the discriminatory policies of such countries as Australia and the United States. The party politicians seemed unable to offer any way out of Japan's difficulties.

In these circumstances, the expansionist foreign policy called for by the radical nationalists seemed, to more and more Japanese, a bold and practical solution to the nation's crisis. The existing colonies of Taiwan and Korea had already brought many benefits. An extension of Japanese territory on the Asian mainland would provide land for settlers, a market for goods and new sources of raw materials. The other great powers had acquired their empires by force of arms. Why should Japan not do likewise? Indeed, Japan, as the only modernized Asian state, could be said to have more right to develop East Asia than any of the Western powers whose culture was so alien and whose homelands were so far away. Many Japanese diplomats and politicians saw the dangers in such a line of policy, but they found themselves increasingly forced to react to initiatives taken by the military, and especially by younger officers whom their seniors were either unable or unwilling to control. The cautious policies of the 1920s seemed, in any case, to have brought Japan few benefits in prestige, prosperity or security.

MANCHUKUO

On the night of 18 September 1931 a small explosion caused slight damage to the track of

18   Divinity on wheels — the emperors Hirohito and Pu Yi in Tokyo, 1935.

19   The Promised Land — a propaganda poster promises emigrants to Manchuria fertile land and a full table. Manchuria, with a population of 30 million, had only half as many people as Japan and was three times as large.

現世樂園

20 Japanese expansion in East Asia, 1895-1933.

the South Manchurian Railway outside Mukden. This act of "sabotage" was almost certainly arranged by Japanese officers and used as an excuse for an attack on the local Chinese garrison, followed by a rapid take-over of the whole of Manchuria. The Japanese government, taken by surprise, was unable to prevent the Kwantung Army from setting up an independent "puppet" state of Manchukuo in March 1932, under its own Manchu emperor, Pu Yi. In reality, the local army commanders were the government, and in 1933 the province of Jehol was added to the new state.

The League of Nations condemned Japan's actions and recommended that Chinese sover-eignty be restored to Manchuria. However, it had no force at its disposal to accomplish this, and the Western powers, distracted by their economic problems, were not inclined to under-take the burden. All that League members could do was refuse to recognize Manchukuo. Japan argued that the area was in such chaos that China was incompetent to protect Japanese rights and property. When this failed to convince the critics, Japan withdrew from the League.

UNREST IN JAPAN

Meanwhile, in Japan itself, the atmosphere of tension was heightened by a series of violent incidents. In 1931 senior army officers just managed to thwart an attempted military coup. In February 1932 a former finance minister and the head of the Mitsui corporation were assassinated. In May 1932 prime minister Inukai was shot. All of the dead had been outspoken opponents of an aggressive foreign policy. Public sympathy for the "selfless" motives of the killers was so great that they received only light sentences. The acquisition of Manchuria had definitely increased the popularity of the military. The conquest itself was seen as a daring and heroic adventure. And it had brought real benefits in terms of employment and a stimulus to the economy. The military were able to use their prestige to demand increased spending on armaments, which also gave a boost to industry. The navy likewise turned to expansion, abandoning the agreements on arms limitation.

On 26 February 1936, 1,400 troops of the elite First Division and Imperial Guards seized key government buildings in Tokyo, and teams of assassins killed ex-prime minister Admiral Saito, the finance minister, the inspector-general of military education and, by mistake, the brother-in-law of the prime minister. The objects of the mutiny were to purge Japan of corruption in high places and to put more radical generals in charge of the army. The coup collapsed when the emperor rejected its leaders' claim that they were acting on his behalf. After a swift and secret trial, the coup leaders were shot and so were a number of civilian extremists who held the same views.

The senior army officers had restored order; but, at the same time, they found themselves able to claim that any policies of which they disapproved should be abandoned, because they might cause unrest among junior officers. This made it much easier for the army to extend its control over many areas of national life. Generals were appointed as heads of civilian ministries. Censorship was made more strict. In education, unthinking nationalism became the order of the day. Shinto traditions were re-modelled to stress the divinity of the emperor. In 1938 the Diet passed a National General Mobilization Law which enabled the government to re-organize industry for war production. In the same year everyone was forced to join a local citizens'

association, which regulated daily life and spread government propaganda.

In some ways Japan in the 1930s resembled the Fascist nations, Germany and Italy, to which it was joined by an Anti-Comintern (anti-Communist) pact of 1936. In all three countries the state imposed its authority on the worlds of work and social life. The superiority of the family and the race over the individual was asserted. Violence was glorified and rule by parliaments – government by discussion — was despised. But Japan was not really a Fascist state in the true sense. There was no "magic" leader like Hitler or Mussolini; public respect in this sense belonged to the emperor alone. There was no mass party committed to revolutionary change — like the Fascists and the Nazis. There was, however, a clear strengthening of military influence, conservative values and traditional authority.

WAR WITH CHINA

In July 1937, following a minor clash, full-scale, but undeclared war broke out between Japan and China. The Japanese feared the possibility of an alliance of Chinese Communists and Nationalists which might unite the country against them. After bitter fighting, the Japanese took Peking, Shanghai and the Chinese capital, Nanking, where a quarter of a million civilians were brutally murdered in an orgy of atrocities. By October 1938 the Japanese held almost all of the coastline, the major cities and most of the north and centre of the country. Chinese resistance continued guerilla-style. Britain and the US, meanwhile, condemned Japan's actions as a violation of the Nine Power Treaty of 1922 but did no more.

THE SECOND WORLD WAR

The outbreak of war in Europe in 1939 led to a general fear among the Japanese military that Germany would take over the British, French and

21 Making friends — a Japanese soldier shares sweets with Chinese children.

22 Making enemies — Chinese victims of Japanese bombing.

23 Prime minister General Tojo and cabinet colleagues,
November 1941.

Dutch colonies in South-East Asia. In June 1940,
therefore, Japan announced the establishment
of a "Greater East Asia Co-Prosperity Sphere", a
vast bloc of countries to be led by Japan in a
new era of economic development. In 1941
Japan forced France's defeated Vichy government to allow Japanese air bases to be established in Indo-China. The United States, which
had long criticized the extension of Japanese
power in East Asia, cut off its exports of oil to
Japan. Without oil, the Japanese could scarcely
hope to advance into South-East Asia or even
to hold their positions in China. US demands
for a complete withdrawal of Japanese troops
from China were, moreover, completely un-
acceptable to the military. Negotiations between

the two governments proved fruitless. The
Japanese refused to give up what they had won
at such great cost. The Americans refused to
accept anything less. Since they could not go
back, the Japanese were forced to go on, well
knowing the risks involved. On 1 December
1941, the final decision in favour of war was
made in Tokyo. The plan was to attack America's
main naval force at a single blow and conquer
South-East Asia before America could re-arm.
Fortified by the oil, tin and rubber of the conquered lands, and secure in established defences,
the Japanese would then challenge America to
launch an attack across the Pacific. Many Japanese generals thought that, while America
might have the means to fight, it did not have
the will to do so. By attacking Pearl Harbor
an hour before the Japanese embassy in Washington managed to decipher the coded official
declaration of war, Japan gave the US all the
will-power it needed.

YOUNG HISTORIAN

A

1 Why did the Japanese become more willing to support extremist policies in the 1930s?

2 Why and how did the power of the military increase in the 1930s?

3 How did Japan come to declare war on the USA?

4 Explain the meaning of (a) cash-crop, (b) discriminatory, (c) expansionist, (d) puppet state, (e) coup, (f) Fascist, (g) guerilla-style.

B

Write a short speech which a Japanese headmaster might have given to school-leavers during the 1930s.

C

Write a series of headlines outlining the main events of the 1930s.

D

Make up a series of slogans to encourage Japanese people to emigrate to Manchuria.

TOTAL WAR 1941–1954

PEARL HARBOR AND OTHER JAPANESE VICTORIES

The Japanese attack on Pearl Harbor on 7 December 1941 was both a brilliant success and a disastrous failure. The strike force, under Admiral Nagumo, was able to approach its target quite undetected. The Americans hourly expected a Japanese attack in the Philippines. Taken off guard, they were unable to offer any more than token resistance, and the Japanese were able to press home their advantage with ferocity and precision. Eighteen American ships were sunk or damaged and more than 300 planes put out of action. The Americans lost 2,400 dead, the Japanese about 100. In fact, the damage was less spectacular than it seemed. Most of the oil tanks, dry docks and repair facilities were unharmed and the three aircraft carriers, the most modern and powerful ships in the US Pacific fleet, were safely at sea on manoeuvres. Had they been destroyed as well, Japan's strategy of a knock-out blow might have worked. But they were not and it did not.

The bombing of Pearl Harbor elated the Japanese and united the Americans. Had Japan continued to press forward in South-East Asia, without directly attacking American forces or territories, it seems possible that public opinion in the United States might have remained divided and uncertain on the issue of war or peace. But the effect of what Roosevelt called "this day of infamy" was to shock America into a sudden unity and prime politicians and people for an all-out war effort. As Admiral Yamamoto, the leading strategist of the Imperial Navy had predicted, Japan was to be crushed by the sleeping giant it had so recklessly awakened. But for a short while, as Yamamoto had also predicted, Japan was to hold the upper hand.

In the five months following Pearl Harbor Japanese forces in South-East Asia and the Pacific won a series of victories unparalleled in military history. The explanation for the repeated defeats suffered by the Allies lies partly in their own incompetence and unpreparedness. In the Philippines, nine hours after Pearl Harbor, American aircraft were destroyed on the ground, lined up wing to wing. A day later the battleship *Prince of Wales* and the battle-cruiser *Repulse*, which had been sent without adequate air-cover to reinforce the British position in the Far East, were sunk by carrier-based Japanese planes. Hong Kong fell on Christmas Day. Six weeks later, having swept through the supposedly "impenetrable" jungles of the Malay peninsula, the Japanese took the "impregnable" fortress of Singapore from the rear. On 15 February 1942 the British garrison surrendered. The Japanese took 73,000 prisoners and shattered British imperial prestige in Asia for ever. By March the Dutch East Indies were completely in Japanese hands. By April American resistance in the Philippines had ended. By June the conquest of Burma had brought Japanese troops to the borders of India. In less than a year Japan had conquered an area stretching 4,000 miles from Sakhalin to New Guinea and 6,000 miles from the Assamese border to the Gilbert Islands. And this conquest was very largely achieved by forces

24   Devastated American ships sunk at anchor, Pearl Harbor, 7 December 1941.

which consisted of less than 200,000 men and fewer than 1,600 planes. On land, the Japanese faced enemies who were more numerous and better equipped. How then can one explain what

one historian has called "the most remarkable military feat of the entire Second World War?" Oxford historian Richard Storry suggests that "the ingredients of Japanese success were surprise, air superiority and matchless fighting spirit", and he emphasizes that, as Churchill himself put it, the Western powers totally under-

Legend on map:
- Under Japanese control July 1942
- Japanese advances

Map labels: RUSSIA, Sakhalin, MANCHURIA, To Aleutians, JAPAN, KOREA, Yenan, CHINA, To Pearl Harbor, Chungking, INDIA (Assam), WAKE ISLAND, BURMA, FRENCH INDO CHINA, Hong Kong, SIAM, PHILIPPINES, GUAM, MALAY PENINSULA, SINGAPORE, BORNEO, NEW GUINEA, DUTCH EAST INDIES, Air raids, AUSTRALIA

25   Japanese advances 1941-42.

estimated "the violence, fury, skill and might of Japan".

Between 1942 and 1944 Japan claimed to be creating its new sort of empire of equals. At the same time, it exploited the economic resources of its conquests, to aid its war effort. There was a basic conflict here. Under the slogan, "Asia for the Asians", Japan claimed to be liberating the continent from Western colonialism and creating, under her leadership, a "Greater East Asia Co-Prosperity Sphere", in which the agricultural economies of East and South-East Asia would gradually be modernized by Japan, which had achieved a full mastery of Western technology. Alongside this, Japan claimed to be preserving Asian cultural traditions and encouraging the

legitimate aspirations of different colonial peoples for independence. In Vietnam and Indonesia local nationalist movements were strengthened by Japanese patronage and eventually achieved independence after the war. In the Philippines, by contrast, local pro-American feelings led to guerilla resistance. Everywhere the strains of war led the Japanese to emphasize economic priorities over the long-term goals of nation-building. The result was widespread forced labour throughout South-East Asia, inflation and food shortages. In these circumstances, slogans about a "Co-Prosperity Sphere" seemed no more than a hypocritical veil to cover naked plunder.

Japanese treatment of prisoners-of-war was often brutal in the extreme. Under-fed, over-worked, subjected to cruel and humiliating punishments, they were often denied even the most basic medical assistance. Tens of thousands died or were permanently crippled in body or mind by their experiences. Yet visitors to Japan have always remarked on the gentleness and warmth of the people, their love of nature and art, and their kindness to strangers. Moreover, there is a striking contrast between the treatment of prisoners in the 1940s and their treatment during the Russo-Japanese war of 1904-5, when the chivalry of the Japanese was praised by many Western correspondents. How can these contradictions be explained?

The American anthropologist, Ruth Benedict, whose book *The Chrysanthemum and the Sword* was written during the Second World War, suggested that Japanese behaviour is regulated by a "situational ethic", which means that rules and ideas about how people should be treated apply to specific groups and specific relationships. Japanese children are brought up with very detailed guidance on the specific way they should behave in their relationships with their teachers, their neighbours, their parents, their employers, and so on. This contrasts with the much vaguer Western-style "universal ethic", which simply indicates certain principles of honesty and justice which individuals should learn to apply in their relations with anyone, whatever circumstances arise. When Japanese, governed by a situational ethic, find themselves in a situation for which no rules already exist, they are thrown back on untrained emotion. Thus Japanese brutality towards prisoners can be explained by the fact that they were foreigners — with whom Japanese had no experience in dealing — and by the fact that these foreigners had surrendered and thus thrown away their honour and manhood as warriors. (Japanese soldiers were given no training in how to behave as prisoners-of-war because it was assumed that they would never surrender. Those who were captured, regarding themselves dead to their former comrades, sometimes actually aided their captors by directing artillery or giving away military information.)

Other explanations of the ill-treatment of prisoners are also possible and need not contradict Ruth Benedict's theory. The Japanese army of the 1930s and 40s was not the army of 1905. Many of its officers came from poor rather than samurai families and may have been eager to assert their right to be officers by behaving in a particularly aggressive way. Many of the recruits were poor peasants and Koreans, bullied by the older and professional soldiers and, therefore, inclined to release their frustrations and anger on the only people beneath them in the pecking order of the army. Also, the army was over-stretched for most of the war, moving rapidly and always short of supplies. Few Japanese soldiers were adequately fed or clothed, and most were driven to the limits of physical endurance, with only the most basic medical care available to cope with wounds, tropical diseases, insect bites and sores. In many instances the prisoners were little worse off than their captors.

THE DEFEAT OF THE JAPANESE

Just as Japan seemed to have gained a decisive advantage, the tide began to turn. In the Battle of the Coral Sea (May 1942) the Japanese tried, and failed, to capture Port Moresby, on the southern coast of New Guinea; the battle also introduced a new style of warfare, being fought entirely between carrier-based planes. A month later the Japanese navy suffered its first major defeat in modern times as it tried to seize the American base on Midway Island. Having cracked the Japanese radio code, the Americans were able to ambush the attackers, who lost 300 planes, 100 crack pilots and 21 ships, including 4 of their best aircraft carriers. News of this disaster was kept from the Japanese public.

After Midway, Japan was on the defensive, facing a two-pronged Allied counter-offensive — one force, under General Douglas MacArthur, driving through the South-West Pacific, from New Guinea to the Philippines, while the other, commanded by Admiral Chester Nimitz, struck through the islands of the central Pacific until it could establish secure bases from which Japan

itself could be bombed into submission.

Everywhere Allied forces met unflinching resistance from Japanese troops willing to die to the last man rather than surrender. The Americans lost 372 men taking Kwajalein, one of the strategically vital Marshall Islands; the defending Japanese garrison suffered a death toll of 7,870. On Saipan, in the Marianas, only 1,000 of the 32,000 defenders were left alive when organized resistance ended in July 1944. Ten thousand civilians also died, and Admiral Nagumo, commander of the fleet which had attacked Pearl Harbor, committed *hara-kiri* (ritual suicide by self-disembowelment) rather than accept the

destroying aircraft factories, airfields and other strategic targets. In March 1945 they began to set fire to whole areas of Japan's sprawling wooden cities. In a single raid on Tokyo, more than 80,000 Japanese civilians were killed, 40,000 wounded and a million made homeless. By the end of the war every major city, except the thousand-year-old cultural capital, Kyoto, had been devastated, half a million Japanese civilians had been killed and 2.5 million homes destroyed.

But it was not death which strangled the Japanese war effort. It was destruction. Women could work in coal-mines and schoolboys in factories, but nothing could replace machinery, worn out by over-use, and nothing could supply the oil, minerals and food lost at sea to American planes and submarines. Every day hunger told the Japanese people what their leaders dared not say — victory was impossible, defeat inevitable. Grimly, they prepared to defend their homes with bamboo spears. These preparations for the ultimate sacrifice emphasized the importance of the warning John Morris (see page 10) had given two years earlier:

I believe it to be of the utmost importance for the war to be brought home to the people of Japan themselves. They know so little of what is happening in the world today, that only when the war is actually brought to their homeland itself will they realize they are beaten. Nothing less than an occupation of the country will be necessary; not necessarily a very long one, but one long enough to make the fact of our victory and their defeat incontestable.

As the Allied forces came nearer to the home islands of Japan, they confronted an ever more desperate resistance. Following the spirit of the medieval samurai, who would rather face death than the dishonour of defeat, squads of suicide pilots were formed. They were called "*Kamikaze*" which means "Divine Wind", the name given to the typhoon which had saved Japan from a Mongol invasion nearly seven hundred years before. But their sacrifice, despite the terrible damage they inflicted on American naval forces

shame of capture. In Burma Japanese forces, starved of supplies and ammunition, fell back before the combined onslaught of Indian, American, British and Nationalist Chinese troops. They left behind them more than 200,000 dead.

From Saipan, American bombers could fly direct to Tokyo. At first, they concentrated on

by deliberately crashing their bomb-laden planes onto the invading ships, was in vain. On 1 April 1945 Okinawa, the last stronghold outside Japan itself, was invaded. By the end of June the Japanese had lost more than 100,000 men in defence of the island; an equal number of civilians had also been killed. In the final two months of the war the combined Anglo-American Third Fleet destroyed or damaged some 3,000 Japanese planes and sank or damaged 1,600 naval and merchant vessels. Japan's military position was now hopeless. But did the Japanese military leaders believe this?

At the outbreak of hostilities, both the British and the Americans had underestimated the strength and skill of the Japanese. The early victories of their foe led them to take a different view and, in every major offensive campaign, they attempted to assure a basic superiority in man-power and weapons. Japanese leaders were less willing to acknowledge the significance of Allied industrial power. Conceding that the Western powers had the edge in science and production, they believed them incapable of the strength of will needed for final victory. Japan might be inferior in arms but not in valour. If necessary, they would fight for a hundred years. Allied awareness of this determination was to lead to the taking of a fateful decision.

Meeting at Potsdam in July 1945, the United States, Britain and China issued a joint declaration calling on Japan to give up all its overseas territories, to disband its armed forces, to hand over its leaders for trial as war criminals, and to accept military occupation and a democratic form of government. Refusal of this offer of "peace, security and justice" would lead to the "prompt and utter destruction" of Japan. The Japanese government responded with the announcement that it would "press forward resolutely to carry the war to a successful conclusion". US President Harry S. Truman, who had succeeded Roosevelt in April, then authorized the use of the atomic bomb, which had been perfected by a joint team of Allied scientists after years of research.

Early on 6 August 1945 the bomber *Enola Gay* took off, carrying a single bomb which would

27 Japanese defeat.

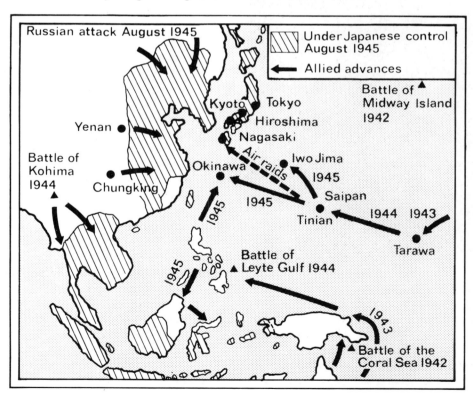

explode with a force equal to 20,000 tons of TNT. At 8.15 am this bomb was dropped on the coastal city of Hiroshima, military headquarters of western Japan. A Japanese history professor, who was three miles away from the blast, later described the sequence of events which followed the dropping of the bomb:

A blinding . . . flash cut sharply across the sky . . . the skin of my body felt a burning heat . . . and then there was a huge 'boom' . . . like the rumbling of distant thunder. At the same time a violent rush of air pressed down my entire body . . . there were some moments of blankness . . . then a complicated series of shattering noises . . . .. I saw many dreadful scenes after that . . . .. But Hiroshima didn't exist — that was mainly what I saw — Hiroshima just didn't exist.

More than 200,000 people were killed or injured, or simply disappeared. Yet the Japanese military leaders were unmoved in their determination to carry on the war. At this point, however, a new factor entered into the calculations of all concerned.

At the Yalta Conference in February 1945 Britain and the USA had received a pledge from the USSR that it would enter the war against Japan "about 90 days" after the surrender of Germany, which came in May. In return, Russia was promised the return of its pre-1904 rights in Manchuria as well as sovereignty over the Kuriles and southern Sakhalin.

In July the Japanese government had approached Russia, regarding the possibility of its intervening to bring about a negotiated peace. Russia's reply, not delivered until 8 August, announced that "from 9 August the Soviet government will consider itself to be at war with Japan". Within hours of this declaration a second atomic bomb destroyed the Japanese city of Nagasaki. On the same day Russian forces invaded Manchuria, Korea and southern Sakhalin.

Even after these disasters the Japanese military remained opposed to surrender, despite pressure from members of the cabinet and Supreme Council. At a special Imperial Conference the emperor intervened to break the deadlock. On 10 August the Japanese government announced

its acceptance of the Potsdam terms, excepting any "demand which prejudices the prerogatives of His Majesty as a sovereign ruler". In its reply the US government stated that "the authority of the emperor and the Japanese government to rule the State shall be subject to the Supreme Commander of the Allied Powers". On 14 August a second Imperial Conference was called. The two Japanese chiefs of staff and the army minister opposed surrender without an explicit guarantee that the emperor's position would be protected. The Prime Minister (Suzuki), the Navy Minister (Yonai), and the Foreign Minister (Togo) saw no alternative but to surrender without conditions. Again the emperor broke the deadlock by supporting the surrender faction. The atomic bombs and the Russian invasion had intensified Japan's crisis to such a degree that only the personal intervention of the emperor could resolve it. It was a supreme irony that only the occupant of the imperial throne had the authority to put its very survival in jeopardy.

In his first ever direct broadcast to his people, the emperor announced the decision to "pave the way for a grand peace for all the generations to come by enduring the unendurable and suffering the unsufferable". This broadcast was followed by the suicide of more than 500 army and naval officers. On 2 September the articles of surrender were signed by representatives of the Japanese government aboard the US battleship *Missouri*, in the presence of General Douglas MacArthur.

The Allied decision to use the atomic bomb has been the subject of controversy ever since. In his *Memoirs*, President Truman wrote:

. . . it had been estimated that it would require until the late fall of 1946 to bring Japan to her knees . . . all of us realized that the fighting would be fierce and the losses heavy . . . .. The final decision of where and when to use the atomic bomb was up to me. Let there be no mistake about it. I regard the bomb as a military weapon and never had any doubt that it should be used. The top military advisers to the President recommended its use, and when I talked to Churchill he unhesitatingly told me that he favoured the use of the atomic bomb if it might aid to end the war.

Roger Makins, secretary of the combined British-American policy committee which gave formal approval to the decision to use the bomb, set out more fully the arguments in favour of this course:

> The position at the end of July was that the Japanese were still fully in the war . . . There was no real indication that the government was prepared to give up fighting or if the government gave in that the Army would . . . the Americans were poised for the invasion of Japan . . . that operation might have cost a million lives. The British were poised to invade Malaya . . . and that certainly would have involved heavy casualties. . . the Europeans were sinking slowly into an economic decline and it was clearly going to be a more difficult task [of reconstruction] the longer the war in the Far East continued. . . . the use of the atomic weapon gave the Japanese . . . a sufficient face-saving reason to enable them to surrender . . .. It was designed to bring the Japanese war to an end and in fact it did so.

Edward Teller, one of the scientists who worked on the atomic bomb, felt, however, that:

> . . . we should have demonstrated it to the Japanese before using it, . . . had the Japanese surrendered after such a demonstration, then a new age would have started in which the power of human knowledge stopped a war without killing a single individual.

In the opinion of the distinguished military writer, Captain Sir Basil Liddell Hart:

> Surrender was already sure and there was no real need to use a weapon under whose dark shadow the world has lived ever since.

Admiral William D. Leahy, Chief of Staff to the American President 1942-9, took the same view:

> . . . the use of this barbarous weapon . . . was of no material assistance . . .. The Japanese were already defeated and were ready to surrender because of the effective sea blockade and the successful bombing of conventional

28 Devastated — Osaka water-front, 1945.

weapons. It was my reaction that the scientists and others wanted to make this test because of the vast sums that had been spent on the project. Truman knew that and so did the other people involved . . .. My own feeling was that in being the first to use it we had adopted the ethical standards common to barbarians in the dark ages.

It should be noted that the unexpectedly sudden ending of the war against Japan fore-stalled the possibility of Russian participation in the occupation of Japanese territories, and that the successful dropping of the atomic bomb served to warn the Soviet government that America now possessed a formidable weapon of terrifying force and destructiveness.

YOUNG HISTORIAN

A
1 Why did Japan attack Pearl Harbor?
2 How can you account for Japan's rapid early successes in the Second World War?
3 Did Japan liberate Asia?
4 Why did Japan surrender?
5 Explain why you would or would not have used the atomic bomb.

B

Imagine you are a Japanese soldier serving in South-East Asia. Write a letter home describing your experiences. (Remember that your officer will censor it.)

C

Write a series of headlines covering the events of the war years (a) from a Japanese point of view, (b) from an American point of view.

D

Draw a map showing: (a) Japan's conquests, (b) the major events leading to its defeat.

OCCUPATION 1945–1952

MACARTHUR AND OCCUPATION POLICY

The occupation of Japan was, in theory, an Allied operation; in practice, the making and enforcement of policy was almost entirely in American hands. Executive power was delegated to General Douglas MacArthur, the Supreme Commander of the Allied Powers (SCAP — a term also applied to the occupation authorities generally). The general objectives which he was to pursue were set out in a document entitled "United States Initial Post-Surrender Policy for Japan":

29   The last shogun — General Douglas MacArthur signs the Japanese instrument of surrender aboard the USS *Missouri*, 1 September 1945.

The ultimate objectives of the United States in regard to Japan . . . are:

(a) To insure that Japan will not again become a menace to the United States or to the peace and security of the world.

(b) To bring about the eventual establishment of a peaceful and responsible government which will respect the rights of other states and will support the objectives of the United States as reflected in the ideals and principles of the Charter of the United Nations.

These objectives will be achieved by the following principal means:

(a) Japan's sovereignty will be limited to the islands of Honshu, Hokkaido, Kyushu, Shikoku and such minor outlying islands as may be determined . . .

(b) Japan will be completely disarmed and demilitarized. The authority of the militarists and the influence of militarism will be totally eliminated . . .

(c) The Japanese people shall be encouraged to develop a desire for individual liberties and respect for fundamental human rights, particularly the freedoms of religion, assembly, speech and the press. They shall also be encouraged to form democratic and representative organizations.

(d) The Japanese people shall be afforded opportunity to develop for themselves an economy which will permit the peacetime requirements of the population to be met.

The occupation objectives may be concisely summarized as demilitarization and democratization. Demilitarization was the first priority. By November 1945 the armed forces had been demobilized and, except for those in Russian hands, had been mostly repatriated to Japan. Democratization involved far more complex and far-reaching reforms, affecting not merely politics

30 **The greatest extent of the Japanese empire, 1945, and its division under the US Initial Post-Surrender Policy for Japan.**

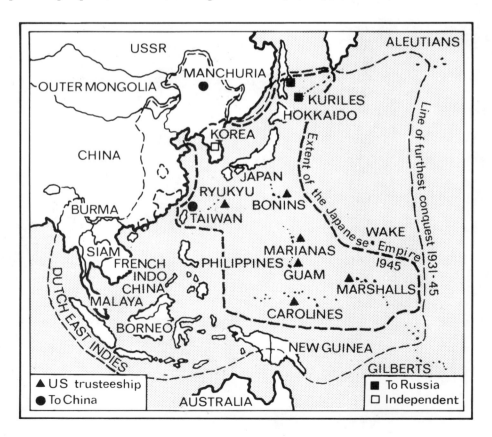

and the law, but the economy and education as well.

Many features of Japanese society seemed hostile to the task of turning the country into a democracy — the people's devotion to their emperor, and their hatred of foreigners encouraged by war-time propaganda and the inability of the occupiers to communicate directly with them in their own language. On the other hand, the Japanese were a highly-educated people whom it was possible to inform through a well-developed press. There were also many political and labour leaders and intellectuals in Japan, who had clung to liberal and democratic ideals despite persecution, and who might form the nucleus of a new political elite. And there was the general disillusionment with the militarists who had brought the nation to its present situation of humiliation and despair. Finally, there was the personality of MacArthur himself, the "American Shogun", theatrical, fearless, firm believer in strong leadership, utterly determined to carry out his mission and convinced of both his ability and his destiny to do so.

In December and January 1946 the machinery of war-time repression and censorship was abolished and an initial purge of militarists begun. Basic reforms in agriculture, education and labour relations and the establishment of a new constitution (see page 54) occupied the rest of 1946 and 1947. From 1948 onwards new emphases in occupation policy became clear. MacArthur had made it plain as early as March 1947 that Japanese acceptance of reform had been so encouraging that the occupation should be brought to an early end. The spread of Communist power in Eastern Europe after 1945 and the rise of Communist power in China also led to a significant reversal of America's attitude of distrust of Japan. Japan was no longer a defeated enemy to be treated with suspicion and disdain, but a budding democracy to be fostered as a valued ally. More and more effective power passed into the hands of the Japanese government. SCAP virtually ceased to initiate reforms and confined its role to one of overall general supervision.

In carrying out his duties, MacArthur had the undoubted advantage of supreme and undisputed authority. There were no Allied zones or partners as in Germany. Japan was effectively isolated from the outside world. SCAP decided which Japanese could leave the country and which foreigners could enter it.

The Japanese authorities were denied any possibility of openly limiting the scope or extent of the Supreme Commander's authority, as his instructions made clear:

> The authority of the emperor and the Japanese government to rule the State is subordinate to you as Supreme Commander . . . . Our relations with Japan do not rest on a contractual basis but on an unconditional surrender.

The occupation brought many startling changes to Japan, but it did not involve a complete break with the past. The changes were, for the most part, put into effect by Japanese officials, and many of them, such as the enlargement of women's rights, represented a continuation of trends which had begun more than a quarter of a century before, or, as in the case of agricultural reform, had long been desired by significant but previously powerless interests. There was, in fact, no realistic option open to the Americans except to work through the existing machinery of the Japanese state, which, despite the collapse of the economy, survived intact. Few Americans had any detailed knowledge of Japan; even fewer were fluent in Japanese.

Of all the institutions of Japan, none was more important than the emperor. Fear of Soviet occupation and social revolution had prompted the Japanese government to surrender to America, in the hope of preserving the emperor system. Some of the Allies wanted to try the emperor as a war criminal and abolish imperial rule altogether. But the advice of more knowledgeable figures prevailed. Joseph C. Grew, US Ambassador to Japan in the 1930s, argued that the emperor alone could guarantee Japanese acceptance of the changes which America intended to bring about. He would stand as a symbol of order and continuity. Any attempt to abolish the imperial office could only lead to violent resistance and social chaos. A peaceful transition to democracy would, in these circumstances, be impossible. As it turned out, the co-operation of the emperor was to prove

invaluable in carrying out the tasks of reform.

Professor Jun Eto has emphasized that

a majority of the Japanese people accepted defeat with unexpectedly good grace. One reason for this reaction may well have been the fact that the command to surrender came directly from the mouth of the Emperor himself. Throughout the war years, the Japanese had fought for the sake of the Emperor. Now that he had personally called on his subjects to lay down their arms . . . it was natural . . . that they should obey his command.

However, the destruction of militarism required more than a mere cessation of hostilities.

MILITARISM ABOLISHED

For two years an Allied International Military Tribunal for the Far East sat in Tokyo, trying top

31 No longer divine — the emperor is now regarded as the symbol of the people's unity and not the source of political authority.

Japanese officers and officials accused of war crimes against humanity. Of the twenty-five tried, seven, including ex-prime minister General Tojo, were hanged and the rest sentenced to prison for from seven years to life. Many of these sentences were later commuted. Individual Allied countries also held trials of Japanese accused of war crimes. Not surprisingly, these proceedings were considered by many Japanese to be "victors' justice", since only nationals from the countries that lost the war were tried and most of the accusations related to offences against Western personnel, rather than against the Chinese or other Asians who suffered far more at the hands of the Japanese.

"Purges" were also carried out, with the aim of removing from positions of leadership persons held responsible for the aggressive policies of the militarist period. As the following table shows, officers of the armed forces and prominent politicians suffered most in the purges, while civil servants and business executives, whose co-operation had, of course, been essential for the prosecution of Japan's war effort, were hardly affected. The power of these two groups was, therefore, enhanced by the continuity of their influence.

Category	Number purged	Percentage of Total
Military	167,035	79.6
Politicians	34,892	16.5
Civil Servants	1,809	0.9
Businessmen	1,898	0.9
Others	4,654	2.1

EDUCATIONAL REFORMS

Commitment to democracy necessarily implied commitment to the ideal of a literate and well-informed citizenry, capable of making rational political choices. Consequently, a wide range of educational reforms was undertaken at the direction of the SCAP authorities. A massive purge of teachers cleared out those who had been ardent supporters of the militarist regime and opened the ranks of the profession to left-wingers who had been previously barred. (A generation later the Japan Teachers' Union remains solidly aligned with the left-wing in Japanese politics.) Teaching methods were reformed, the emphasis being placed on training students *how* to think rather than *what* to think. Text books were re-written to eliminate nationalist propaganda. In an attempt to make education accessible to all, compulsory school attendance was lengthened from six to nine years for all boys and girls, and a University was established in each of the prefectures into which Japan was divided. Article 26 of the new constitution decreed that "All people shall have the right to receive an equal education correspondent to their ability" and that compulsory education should be free. However, many Japanese thought that the extension of educational opportunities was achieved only at the cost of lowering standards.

TRADE UNIONS

The encouragement of trade unions was another aspect of the democratization process. It was believed that vigorous and effective unions would help urban workers become involved in politics and would act as a countervailing force against the influence of big business. A trade union law of December 1945 gave workers the right to organize, bargain and strike, and a Labour Relations Board was set up to enforce the act. (These rights were later guaranteed by Article 28 of the new constitution.) Within a year trade union membership had grown from one million to 4.5 million, and by 1949 to 6.5 million. The effectiveness of the unions was limited, however, by the inexperience of their leaders and members, and the occupation authorities soon became concerned that they were falling increasingly under the influence of left-wingers, who seemed more interested in political demonstrations than in industrial negotiations. In 1948 the right to strike was limited by law. In 1950 Communist leaders were driven from the unions in a so-called "red-purge".

AGRICULTURE

The largest single category of Japanese workers was not factory operatives but small farmers. At the end of the war about 46 per cent of Japanese arable land was worked by tenants who paid their rent by turning over a sizeable portion of their harvest to their landlord.

The occupation authorities' land reform was motivated by a twin desire to diminish the power of the landlords, especially absentees, whom they regarded as a "feudal" and therefore anti-democratic influence, and to create a class of prosperous owner farmers with a vested interest in supporting the new regime which had given them control of the land upon which they depended for their livelihood. The land reform legislation of 1946 forbade anyone to own more than 2½ acres unless they cultivated it themselves, in which case the limit was 7½ acres. (In under-populated Hokkaido the limits were higher.) All surplus land was bought by the government at 1939 prices and resold to farmer tenants who bought it with the vastly inflated 1947 currency. In effect, this boiled down to virtual confiscation.

As a result of the land reform, some 5 million acres of arable land were redistributed to nearly as many tenant farmers, rents in kind virtually disappeared, rent levels generally were much reduced and only about 10 per cent of the cultivated area was still left to be worked by tenants. On the negative side, the land reform froze the pattern of farming in small and scattered plots, and, while giving the farmer the incentive to improve what was now his own land, did little to give him the necessary means.

INDUSTRY

In 1946 the "big four" *zaibatsu*, Mitsui, Mitsubishi, Sumitomo and Yasuda, accounted for a

quarter of the paid-up capital of all incorporated business in Japan, and for much higher proportions of the nation's heavy industry (32.4 per cent) and finance (49.7 per cent).

According to the head of the US Mission on Japanese Countries:

> Whether or not individual Zaibatsu were warmongers is relatively unimportant; what matters is that the Zaibatsu system has provided a setting favourable to military aggression.

It was also alleged that the zaibatsu had held down wages, restricted the development of small businesses, and prevented the emergence of free trade unions with the result that

> in the absence of such groups there has been no economic basis for independence in politics

32 The first woman executive of Kanebo Cosmetics Sales Company. "After the war two things became stronger — women and nylon stockings" (see page 75) — but in politics the proverb has still to come true.

> nor much development of the conflicting interests and democratic and humanitarian sentiments which elsewhere serve as counterweights to military designs.

The original intention was to break the power of these industrial giants by dissolving the holding companies which co-ordinated their activities, selling off many of their assets to small and medium enterprises. In practice, however, other reforms were given priority over the immensely complex task of restructuring Japanese industry and finance, and, by the time the occupation authorities were in a position to begin the process,

52

American attitudes had changed sharply. With the emergence of "Cold War" rivalries with Russia and China, the emphasis was now on building up Japan's economic strength; and thus the industrial giants were allowed to re-establish themselves, even though the power of the individual families over them was broken.

CONCLUSION

There was nothing inevitable about Japan's transition to democracy and prosperity. Exhausted by the strains of combat, disorganized by the assaults of its conquerors, and stunned by the shock of defeat, Japan might easily have turned in another direction had it not been occupied by a strong and self-confident America. Japan had the potential both for democracy — an established tradition of parliamentary, constitutional government going back to 1889 — and for totalitarianism — a genius for collective effort and national co-ordination. Had Japan been occupied by the Soviet Union, it might well have become a dynamic Communist state. Had it been split into separate zones of occupation, its subsequent history might have been as tense and tragic as that of divided Korea. That the occupation preserved elements of the Japanese past as well as setting the nation on a new path is a tribute both to the resilience and discipline of the Japanese and to the self-confidence and idealism of the Americans.

YOUNG HISTORIAN

A

1 Why was the occupation of Japan almost exclusively an American affair? Why did the Americans choose to implement their reforms indirectly through the Japanese administration?

2 Why did the democratization of Japan involve educational and economic changes?

3 Explain the meaning of (a) sovereignty, (b) demobilized, (c) repatriated, (d) absentee landlords.

4 Why was it easier to reform Japanese agriculture than Japanese industry?

B

1 A fortnight elapsed between Japan's surrender and the arrival of the occupation forces. Imagine you were a Japanese living at that time. Write a series of diary entries expressing your hopes and fears for the immediate future.

2 Imagine you are a reporter working for a Japanese newspaper in a medium-sized town. The year is 1952 and the Americans are leaving. Write an article summarizing the changes which have occurred under their influence since 1945.

C

1 Write a series of headlines announcing the major events of the occupation period.

2 Imagine you had the opportunity to meet General MacArthur. What three questions would you most have wished to ask him?

D

Design a poster encouraging Japanese workers to join a trade union.

DEMOCRACY-JAPANESE STYLE

THE SHOWA CONSTITUTION

The democratization of Japan necessarily required the establishment of a democratic constitution which would provide the framework for a more open style of politics. When the Japanese government suggested what the Americans regarded as a series of rather minor revisions to the existing constitution, the initiative was taken out of their hands and an entirely new constitution was drafted, in just over a week, by a small working-party of SCAP officials. It was this document which, after a few small amendments, was adopted by the Diet and became operative on 3 May 1947.

The "Showa Constitution" consists of a preamble and 103 articles, divided into eleven chapters. The preamble states clearly that "sovereign power resides with the people". However, the first chapter of the constitution is devoted not to the rights of the people, but to the position of the emperor, an indirect acknowledgement of the continuing importance of this office, though stripped of all power. Article 1 states: "The Emperor shall be the symbol of the State and of the unity of the people", and Article 4 explicitly affirms that "he shall not have powers relating to government". Chapter II consists solely of Article 9, a unique provision found in no other constitution in the world:

Aspiring sincerely to an international peace based on justice and order, the Japanese people forever renounce war as a sovereign right of the nation and the threat or use of force as a means of settling international disputes.

In order to accomplish the aim of the preceding paragraph, land, sea, and air-forces, as well as other war potential, will never be maintained. The right of belligerency of the state will not be recognized.

The existence of Article 9 has had most significant consequences for the development of Japan's post-war foreign policy (see page 83).

Chapter III, outlining "Rights and Duties of the People", is the longest section, consisting of Articles 10 to 40. The tone, and sometimes the actual wording, echoes closely the sentiments of the constitution of the United States. Article 13 decrees that:

All of the people shall be respected as individuals. Their right to life, liberty and the pursuit of happiness shall, to the extent that it does not interfere with the public welfare, be the supreme consideration in legislation and in other governmental affairs.

Article 14 establishes equality before the law and abolishes the peerage. Article 15 guarantees "universal adult suffrage" and secrecy of the ballot. Article 20 guarantees freedom of religion and orders that "no religious organization shall receive any privileges from the State nor exercise any political authority", and bans the State "from religious education or any other religious activity". (This article was clearly aimed at preventing any possible resurgence of the cult of

State Shinto, with its veneration of the emperor.)

Article 24 is of considerable interest as it makes equality between the sexes a part of the basic law of the land:

> Marriage shall be based only on the mutual consent of both sexes and it shall be maintained through mutual co-operation with the equal rights of husband and wife as a basis.

> With regard to choice of spouse, property rights, inheritance, choice of domicile, divorce and other matters pertaining to marriage and the family, laws shall be enacted from the standpoint of individual dignity and the essential equality of the sexes.

The other chapters set out the powers and

33 Constitutional monarchy — the emperor and empress at a formal session of the Diet.

functions of the various organs of government. The most important provisions were as follows:
— the powerful bodies, such as the Privy Council, and the various civil and military officials who had enjoyed privileged access to the emperor in the pre-war period were either abolished or made subordinate to the Cabinet.
— the Cabinet was to be drawn from the party or coalition which had a majority in the Diet; its authority, like a British Cabinet, rested, therefore, on retaining the confidence of a freely elected parliament.

34 Separation of powers? — in the foreground the National Diet, Japan's legislature; in the background Kasumigaseki and the towering office-blocks of the permanent civil service.

— both houses of the Diet became fully elective; the balance of power between them was shifted decisively in favour of the lower house.

— the judiciary was made independent of the government and the Supreme Court was given the power to decide whether new legislation was constitutional or not.

— governors of prefectures were made subject to election and local government was given increased powers.

Assessments of the Showa Constitution naturally vary. According to American political scientist, Robert E. Ward,

on the basis of text alone, it is a considerably more democratic document than is the Constitution of the United States. The Constitution is also a workable document, although it has flaws and does create problems. For example, any pronounced degree of local autonomy is probably impractical in Japan, judicial review has not proved particularly meaningful in practice and some of the more ambitious civil and human rights and freedoms envisaged in Chapter II of the Constitution will probably long remain pious hopes rather than social or legal facts.

But he concludes that:

the fact that the 1947 Constitution stands unchanged, given its antecedents and the enormous political changes it imposed on a reluctant Japanese leadership — this is perhaps the most remarkable phenomenon of all.

Professor Jun Eto is more critical. To him, the constitution "bears the unmistakeable imprint of the Occupation policy" and therefore the Japanese have

lost a sense of close identity with the various new concepts embodied in the Constitution although they hold favourable feelings toward them . . .. Nor can they enjoy the satisfying

57

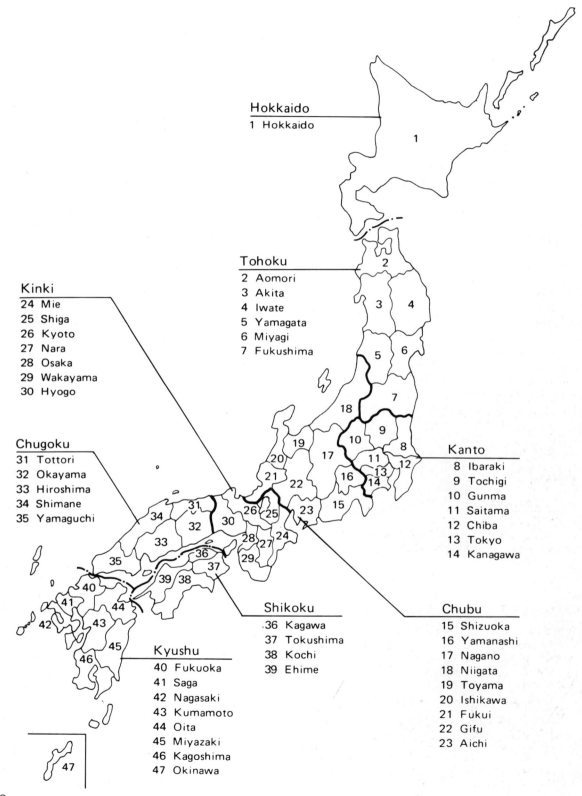

Hokkaido
1 Hokkaido

Tohoku
2 Aomori
3 Akita
4 Iwate
5 Yamagata
6 Miyagi
7 Fukushima

Kinki
24 Mie
25 Shiga
26 Kyoto
27 Nara
28 Osaka
29 Wakayama
30 Hyogo

Chugoku
31 Tottori
32 Okayama
33 Hiroshima
34 Shimane
35 Yamaguchi

Kanto
8 Ibaraki
9 Tochigi
10 Gunma
11 Saitama
12 Chiba
13 Tokyo
14 Kanagawa

Shikoku
36 Kagawa
37 Tokushima
38 Kochi
39 Ehime

Chubu
15 Shizuoka
16 Yamanashi
17 Nagano
18 Niigata
19 Toyama
20 Ishikawa
21 Fukui
22 Gifu
23 Aichi

Kyushu
40 Fukuoka
41 Saga
42 Nagasaki
43 Kumamoto
44 Oita
45 Miyazaki
46 Kagoshima
47 Okinawa

feeling of having won by themselves the various values which the state is supposed to guarantee.

Nevertheless, despite the fact that the Japanese text reads like an awkward translation from the English and does not, therefore, "feel" Japanese, no serious attempts have been made to revise the constitution and it is not, in itself, a major political issue. Japanese politicians have indeed learned to play the game by a new set of rules. And, undoubtedly, the most successful players have been those conservatives who were among the loudest critics of the constitution when it was first promulgated.

JAPANESE POLITICAL LIFE

The immediate post-war years were marked by confusion on the political scene. All the major pre-war parties were revived and dozens of tiny new groupings also appeared; together with numerous independent candidates, these new-comers won more than a third of the votes in the 1946 election. By the 1947 election, however, the major parties had recruited most of these fringe politicians into their ranks and seemed set to dominate the nation's political life once more.

At first, the two conservative parties, the Liberals (formerly the Seiyukai, now the Jiyuto) and the Democrats (formerly the Minseito, now the Minshuto), competed with each other, and the Democrats joined the Socialists to form a coalition government under the Socialist leader, Katayama. Although it passed a number of social and economic reforms, the coalition proved unworkable and the government fell after less than a year in office. Katayama was succeeded by Yoshida, the Liberals' leader, who had already served as prime minister in 1946-47. Yoshida strengthened his position by calling an election and winning an outright majority in the Diet. He remained prime minister until December 1954.

Yoshida, during the pre-war period, had been a consistent supporter of close ties between Japan, Britain and the USA. He had refused the post of ambassador to Washington in 1932 on account of his opposition to Japan's invasion of Manchuria. In 1945 he was imprisoned because he favoured a negotiated peace with the Allies. As prime minister during the occupation period, Yoshida saw his policies as being not a matter of collaborating with a former enemy but of re-establishing links with Japan's natural allies. A committed supporter of big business, he was strongly anti-Communist.

Between 1955 and 1960 the division sharpened between the conservative parties and their main opponents, the Socialists. In 1955, shortly after the left and right wings of the Socialist party had re-united, the Liberals and the Democrats, in response to the threat of a common rival, merged to form the Liberal-Democratic Party. This party has governed Japan ever since. As the 2 re-united parties closed ranks, the tensions between them increased. There were profound disagreements between the two parties over matters of policy as Hatayama, Yoshida's successor as prime minister, attempted to reverse some of the SCAP reforms and re-establish greater central control over the police, education and local government. He also favoured revision of the constitution and a build-up of the armed forces. Unable to defeat these measures in the Diet, the Socialists resorted to street demonstrations.

Confrontation between the two sides reached a climax over the revision of the Security Treaty with the United States in 1960. The Socialists wished to scrap the treaty altogether; the conservatives wished to take advantage of the more favourable terms offered by the United States. After massive public demonstrations against treaty revision, a renewed treaty was at last ratified and Japanese politics entered a new and more tranquil era. One reason for this was the increasing evidence of rising prosperity; whatever else the conservatives might have done, they had made most Japanese better off than anyone had thought possible. Foreign praise for rising living standards gave the Japanese pride in their national achievement.

The LDP's long tenure of political office has enabled it to develop close links with organized business, in the shape of the Keidanren (Federation of Economic Organizations), and with the civil service. Big business supplies most of the election funds for the LDP and a number of the party's top leaders are recruited from the biggest companies. Some of the most able civil servants move into the LDP when they retire; others are taken on by big business. Top politicians, civil servants and businessmen "speak the same language", they have similar educational backgrounds and often find themselves working together on the same committees and study-groups. They

have, for the most part, given the Japanese voter what he has wanted — higher living standards.

The opposition in Japan has been lively but fragmented. The main opposition party is the Japan Socialist Party (JSP), which is critical of big business and the American alliance and influential in the trade union movement. The Democratic Socialist Party (DSP) is a moderate splinter-group which broke away from the JSP. The other main opposition groups are the Japan Communist Party (JCP), which draws much support from students, intellectuals and labour leaders, and the Komeito (Clean Government Party), whose members are largely drawn from the ranks of the Soka Gakkai, a Buddhist religious sect which has opposed corruption in Japan's

36 A free press, safeguard of democracy — practically every Japanese household subscribes to a daily newspaper.

37　Public demonstrations show the right of free speech in action. This loudspeaker van proclaims the message of a right-wing nationalist organization.

During the 1970s a number of observers began to detect important changes in Japan's political life, affecting not only the major political issues but also the institutions and participants involved. Questions of incomes and living standards seemed to become less pressing; nearly everyone was better off. What mattered were environmental issues — noise, traffic congestion, clean air, access to sunlight and open

political life. Other important critics of the authorities are the Federation of Student Unions (Zengakuren), the main trades union confederation (Sohyo) and the press.

space. More and more housewives and young
professional people — the sort of voters who had
never troubled previous governments — seemed
to involve themselves in grass-roots organizations,
campaigning against the effects of uncontrolled
economic growth on town and countryside. The
focus of conflict shifted from national elections
to the municipal and prefectural level, because
it was here, the voters sensed, that effective action
could be taken to curb the power of big business
to pursue its own ends regardless of their impact
on society. Opposition to new industrial develop-

38 Government by persuasion? — electioneering
politicians address the TV cameras as well as the crowds
in the street.

ment was not always successful; sometimes it
was not even particularly sensible. But the fact
that it was taking place showed that Japanese
democracy had entered an important new phase,
in which ordinary citizens were prepared to take
the initiative over issues of immediate concern
to themselves, and their families.

62

YOUNG HISTORIAN

A

1. In what ways is the Showa Constitution more democratic than its predecessor?
2. What do the provisions of the Constitution tell you about American attitudes to Japanese society as it existed before 1945?
3. Why do you think the LDP has been able to stay in power for so long?
4. Explain the meaning of (a) preamble, (b) belligerency, (c) spouse, (d) domicile, (e) autonomy, (f) grass-roots.

B

Write a series of headlines which cover the most important political developments in Japan since 1945.

C

Write a letter to a Japanese newspaper explaining the changes you would most like to see in Japan's political system.

D

1. Design a poster opposing further industrial developments in Japan.
2. Draw a diagram showing how the main elements in the Japanese system of government are related to one another.

THE ECONOMIC MIRACLE

Japan's economic situation in 1945 appeared to be perilous. The loss of its overseas territories had deprived it of the access to energy supplies and raw materials which it had so painfully secured. The repatriation of overseas settlers and officials added some seven million persons to the population. The rapid demobilization of the armed forces led to further disorganization of the labour market. Allied bombing had destroyed some 700,000 houses in Tokyo alone and flattened large areas of every major city, except Kyoto, as well as inflicting substantial damage to railways, ports, factories and shipyards.

Economic recovery was at first extremely hesitant. Soaring inflation, labour unrest, a flourishing black market and the threatened attack on the zaibatsu inhibited planning for the future. In 1947 production was still only 37 per cent of its pre-war level and imports of American food aid were necessary to save the population from outright starvation.

From 1948 SCAP began to foster the economic recovery of Japan, curbing militancy and ending the export of industrial plant to South-East Asia which had been taking place by way of reparations. In 1949 the unpopular "Dodge Plan", a package of taxes and credit restrictions, was imposed, to bring inflation under control.

Then came the Korean war. Between 1950 and 1953 $4,000 million-worth of military procurement orders were placed in Japan. By 1955 production levels were back where they had been in 1936. In 1960 Prime Minister Ikeda announced that Japan would double the average real income of its inhabitants within a decade. Western experts declared this aim hopelessly

unrealistic. It was achieved by 1967, and not until the oil-price crisis of 1973 did Japan's breakneck growth receive any serious check. During the quarter century 1948-73 Japan's GNP in real terms (i.e. allowing for inflation) grew by ten times, a figure 2.5 times as high as the world average.

Growth was accompanied by a transformation of the structure of the Japanese economy. Agriculture shrank into insignificance in terms of its contribution to employment and national output, though its political and strategic importance scarcely diminished. Industry became capital-intensive, dependent upon the most advanced technologies, and acquired a reputation for turning out products which were cheap, reliable and of the highest quality. Textiles lost their former precedence to steel, ships, vehicles, electrical products and precision engineering. Above all, there was a rapid growth in the service

Changes in the structure of the Japanese economy.
A = percentage of total labour force employed.
B = percentage share of Gross Domestic Product.

	Agriculture, Forestry, Fisheries		Mining, Manufacturing, Transport		Services, Transport	
	A	B	A	B	A	B
1955	27.6	23.0	24.4	28.5	38.1	48.5
1960	30.2	14.9	28.0	36.3	41.8	48.9
1965	23.5	11.3	31.9	36.1	44.6	52.6
1970	17.4	7.7	35.2	38.6	47.4	53.7
1975	12.7	6.6	35.2	35.9	52.0	57.5

The price of the miracle? — 39 (above) traffic jams clog the streets of Tokyo, the average cross-town speed being 7 miles per hour; 40 (below) an international gathering of experts considers the problem of pollution.

International Symposium
on
ENVIRONMENTAL DISRUPTION IN THE MODERN WORLD
8-14 March 1970

industries which, by 1975, employed more labour than agriculture and industry added together. Commentators hailed Japan's emergence as a "post-industrial" state, in which knowledge had supplanted physical capital as the key resource, and the data-bank and the research laboratory had replaced the factory as the focus of productive effort.

THE REASONS FOR THE MIRACLE

How can Japan's astonishing economic growth be explained? No single explanation can account for it, but the many factors that combined together can be grouped into three broad categories — (a) those that relate to the general nature of Japanese society, (b) those that relate to governmental policies, and (c) those that relate to

41 A miniature combine harvester in action — the rising cost of labour has hastened the spread of mechanization in the countryside.

favourable international circumstances.

(a) The quality of Japan's labour force has been widely admired by its industrial competitors. The major companies' system of "life-time employment" guarantees the worker job and income security and a wide range of fringe benefits, such as housing and holidays, medical and dental care and low-interest loans. Employees, tied for their entire working lives to the fortunes of a single concern, give it their loyalty and understand clearly that higher wages and bonuses (paid twice a year and amounting to 2-4 months basic wages) can only come out of higher production, sales and profits. Unions are mostly organized on a company, rather than an industry-wide basis; inter-union conflicts and "demarcation disputes" are, in this case, virtually unknown. Strikes do take place, usually in the spring, when the annual round of wage negotiations occurs, but they are rarely long or damaging. Production is, therefore, seldom disrupted, management can plan ahead with confidence and customers are not inconvenienced by unfilled orders or late deliveries.

Japanese managers have not only been able to count on workers who were diligent, loyal and well-educated. They were also able, at least until the mid-1960s, to assume that there were plenty of them. With a steadily rising population overall, the increasing desire of women to find paid employment, and the availability of surplus agricultural labour, released from farm-work by the rapid spread of mechanization, Japanese industry was free of bottlenecks in its labour supply until the mid-1960s. Then a labour shortage began to appear, aggravated by the tendency of more and more young people to stay on at school and college rather than move straight into work.

"Cheap labour" has often been alleged to be the secret of Japan's success. This may have been a factor in the late 1940s and early 1950s, when wages were low, capital was scarce and managers were giving top priority to re-equipping and investing in new technology. But by the late 1960s the average Japanese industrial worker was being paid more than his British or Italian counterpart, and by the 1970s Japanese companies were establishing themselves in South Wales and the North of England, attracted by what was now, to them, the cheap labour available in these areas.

Capital to finance Japan's high rate of industrial investment came chiefly from the major banks, backed by the Bank of Japan itself. The banks acted as a sort of financial vacuum-cleaner, sucking up the savings of the small investor and making them available to industry for investment in new plant and technology. Personal savings levels in Japan are much higher than in Britain (the Japanese worker saves three times as much of his income), probably because fewer benefits are provided by the state in the field of medicine, education and social security.

Perhaps the major reason why Japan achieved rapid economic growth was that it was what the Japanese wanted most. At first, the motivation was simply one of survival; at the end of the war even the most basic necessities were in short supply. But economic growth seemed also to offer a way of building a new Japan, free from the shadows of the past, a Japan whose achievements represented the results of their own effort, initiative and enterprise.

(b) As we have seen, the trend towards economic recovery began with SCAP encouragement and was fostered by reforms in agriculture and education. But government-industry co-operation became even closer as the occupation ended and the big-business-backed Liberal-Democratic Party established itself firmly in power. For the next twenty years government policies were largely to reflect the objectives and priorities of the business community. Taxes on business profits were kept low, and restrictions on the siting and operation of industries kept to a minimum. Tariff barriers and import regulations kept foreign rivals at arms-length from the massive Japanese domestic market. And squabbles between the great industrial corporations over access to new technologies and new markets were often sorted out in the offices of the Japanese Ministry of International Trade and Industry (MITI).

(c) International circumstances also tended to favour Japan's economic recovery. The rapid expansion of world trade and the ready availability of cheap energy and raw materials gave Japanese industry both the incentive and the means to produce and export. The Vietnam war had a similar effect to the Korean war in stimulating Japanese industry through military procurement orders. At the same time, however, Japan's reliance on the USA for its defence enabled it to keep its own spending in this area to less than 1 per cent of GNP, compared with 5 per cent or more for its European rivals, releasing the surplus saved for more productive investment.

THE PRICE OF THE MIRACLE

However, Japan's economic miracle had been achieved at a price. As the Japanese themselves

began to realize around the late 1960s, the environmental costs have been enormous, both in terms of actual damage to landscape and coastlines and in terms of neglect of urban amenities.

Air pollution has been caused by noxious effluents from industrial plants and uncontrolled motor-exhaust fumes.

Pollution of rivers and fishing grounds has been caused by waste-products from mines and chemical works. This has resulted in damage to agriculture and fishery and led to the crippling and death of hundreds of innocent people through mercury and cadmium poisoning.

Housing has been gravely neglected, as has the provision of public parks, libraries and leisure facilities.

Inadequate spending on roads, coupled with a phenomenal increase in the volume of motor traffic, has led to more than 300,000 road deaths since the war — more than the total numbers killed at Hiroshima and Nagasaki added together.

During the 1970s Japanese opinion began to turn against the notion of growth at all costs. The new emphasis was on the "quality of life" and a renewed search for harmony between man and nature. The 1973 oil-price rise made government and business leaders suddenly aware of how dangerously dependent Japan had become on the rest of the world for its basic supplies of energy and raw materials. Growing competition from newly-industrialized Korea and Taiwan, excess capacity in ship-building and steel-making, rising wage-costs, and increasing pressure from Japan's trading partners for it to import more manufactured goods from them, all pointed towards a need to revise the economic formula which had proved so successful for a whole generation. In an era of rising energy costs, rapidly changing technologies, fluctuating currencies and precarious markets, Japanese business would need all of its proven inventiveness and adaptability to survive. At the same time, widespread popular opposition to the spread of nuclear power and the rapid ageing of the

population (20 per cent of all Japanese would be in the 65+ age bracket by 2000 AD) suggested that, even as the problems of further economic development became more acute, the range of options open to policy-makers would become more and more confined by the fears and needs of a well-informed but increasingly sceptical electorate.

43 Waste not — recycling newspapers in the interests of ecology.

YOUNG HISTORIAN

A

1 Why has Japan's post-war economic recovery been called a "miracle"?

2 Why does Japan need to have a highly educated labour force?

3 Why did the Japanese begin to have second thoughts about the desirability of economic growth?

4 Why was the 1973 "oil shock" so serious for Japan?

5 Explain the meaning of (a) militancy, (b) reparations, (c) procurement, (d) capital-intensive, (e) demarcation.

B

1 Compare the working conditions and way of life of a worker in Japanese industry with those of a worker in British industry.

2 Conduct a survey in your school or neighbourhood to find out (a) how many people own Japanese products, (b) what people think about Japanese products.

C

1 Imagine you are a foreign journalist visiting Japan in 1945, 1955 and 1975. Write a series of brief articles describing the condition of the economy.

2 Make up a slogan for a conservation campaign against further industrial development in Japan.

D

1 Draw a map of Japan and mark in the most important industrial areas.

2 Draw a map of the world and mark in the areas (a) to which Japan exports most, (b) from which Japan imports most.

JAPAN TRANSFORMED?

A Japanese Rip van Winkle who fell asleep in 1945 and woke up in 1980 might be forgiven for thinking that he was no longer in the same country. The pace and extent of the changes which have taken place in post-war Japan can be said to amount to a social transformation. The frugal life-style of the 1930s has been replaced by one of lavish material comfort. Television and the motor car have revolutionized the daily lives of the people. The typical worker is no longer a mud-spattered farmer, but an immaculately-suited white collar "salaryman". The kimono is reserved for special occasions, and Western foodstuffs such as meat and dairy products have become a normal feature of the nation's everyday diet. Democracy, women's rights, a massive leisure industry and an even

more massive educational establishment all distinguish the Japan of the 1980s from the Japan of the 1930s. And, for more than half of the population, this sort of Japan is the only one they have ever known.

A foreign visitor, on the other hand, might be more aware of the continuities with the past that underlie the avalanche of changes which have both disconcerted and delighted the older generation of Japanese since 1945. Equality of opportunity may be the ideal and, to a large extent, the reality, in education, employment and politics; but the way the system actually works seems still to favour men over women and the old over the young. A strong sense of hierarchy survives into the democratic age, reinforced by and expressed in formal etiquette

Changes in post-war agriculture

	1960	1975
Total number of farm households (000)	6,057	4,953
Total farm population (000)	34,411	23,195
Total farm population in farm work (000)	14,542	7,907
(of which males)	5,995	2,975
Area planted to rice (000 hectares)	3,308	2,764
Rice production in year (000 tons)	219	29
Area planted to wheat (000 hectares)	602	90
Wheat production in year (000 tons)	1,531	241
Milk cows (000)	824	1,787
Pigs (000)	1,918	7,684
Horses (000)	673	43
Hens and chickens (000)	52,153	242,163

Changes in post-war industry

Energy Supplies (10 thousand million kilocalories)	1955	1965	1975
Total	56,011	165,614	363,031
Imported	13,431	109,577	321,314
Imported petroleum	8,715	82,368	247,159
Atomic	—	9	6,150

Iron and Steel Production (000 tons)	1950	1965	1975	1978
Pig-iron	2,233	27,502	86,877	78,589
Crude steel	4,839	41,161	102,313	102,105

Manufactured Goods	1960	1965	1975	1978
Passenger cars	165,094	696,176	4,567,854	5,975,968
Passenger cars exported	13,704	n.a.	1,857,882	3,166,076
Steel vessels (000 gross tons)	1,759	5,527	15,227	6,295
Desk-top electronic calculators (000)	—	4	30,040	42,319
Radios (000)	12,851	22,937	14,283	16,278
Televisions (000)	3,578	4,190	12,453	13,927
Average monthly hours worked per worker	207	192	168	n.a.

Changes in post-war transport

	1955	1965	1975
Passenger-kilometres	136,112	255,640	323,800
Freight ton-kilometres	43,254	57,298	47,347
Number of trucks owned	1,321,601*	2,870,249	7,381,024
Number of passenger cars owned	440,417*	1,877,912	14,822,093
Ocean vessels (over 3,000 tons in 000 tons)	2,733	10,317	33,547
Tankers (000 tons)	584	4,217	17,646
Total ocean freight carried (000 tons)	87,433	314,166	904,324
Coastal freight carried (000 tons)	59,152	179,654	377,342
Coastal freight in wooden vessels (000 tons)	33,909	43,971	15,528
Overseas exports (000 tons)	3,913	10,213	34,074
Overseas imports (000 tons)	20,797	118,144	415,567
International air passengers carried (000)	101*	436	2,555
International air cargo (ton-km)	13,432*	66,145	772,570

* 1960 figures

and honorific language. Four fifths of Japanese employees still prefer a paternalistic boss, "who may force one to work hard, even to the extent of sometimes bending work rules, but who shows an active concern for one's welfare in private matters outside the job". Traditional attitudes, like traditional customs and pastimes, are not abandoned but find a new place in a way of life that is both more dynamic and more diverse. The essentially Japanese character of Japanese culture and society cannot be undermined by the impact of Western ideas, technologies and fashions, so long as Japan remains the only nation of 100 million people who are all of the same ethnic stock and all speak the same, unique language. This great fact alone guarantees that tradition will remain as an active force shaping social change.

POPULATION

Since 1945 Japan's population can be said to have grown, moved and aged. The total population has expanded from 72 million to 116 million, an increase which can be attributed largely to a dramatic fall in the death rate (from 12.7 per 1,000 persons in 1947-49 to 6.3 in 1975), caused by lower infant mortality and the virtual disappearance of epidemic diseases and tuberculosis.

Rural-urban migration has been a general trend for the last century and has shown little sign of slackening in the post-war period. Between 1925 and 1975 the population in the three metropolitan areas of Tokyo, Osaka and Nagoya increased by 2.6 times, until it came to account for 45 per cent of the total population. Nevertheless, large numbers of the migrants continue, even after two or three generations, to keep up their connection with a village they regard as "home".

The combined effect of continued urbanization, a fall in the birth rate (33.6 per 1,000 in 1947-49, 17.1 by 1975), and a significant increase in the proportion of the population over 65 years of age (8.1 per 1,000 by 1975) has been to bring about a radical change in the size of

Japanese households. In 1950 there were only 889,000 single-person households and 6,304,000 consisting of 6 persons or more; by 1975 the figures were 4,285,000 and 3,256,000 respectively. The old ideal of the multi-generation family of grandparents, parents and children under the same roof is nowadays seldom to be found.

Population

	000s	Average annual rate of increase (%)	Population density (persons per square km)
1880	36,649	0.7	96
1890	39,902	0.9	105
1900	43,847	1.0	115
1910	49,184	1.2	129
1920	55,963	1.3	147
1930	64,450	1.5	169
1940	71,933	0.8	188
1945*	72,147	0.2	196
1950	84,115	2.8	226
1955	90,077	1.4	242
1960	94,302	0.9	253
1965	99,209	1.0	266
1970	104,665	1.1	281
1975	111,940	1.2	300
1978	115,174	0.9	309

*Excludes Okinawa

Ninety per cent of Japanese now consider themselves to be "middle-class". To the Japanese, then, their society does not seem to be split by any great division between rich and poor. Figures for the ownership of consumer durables support the view that in Japan the fruits of affluence have been widely distributed. By 1975 more than 90 per cent of Japanese households possessed a colour television set, a washing machine, a refrigerator and a vacuum cleaner. The contrast with the poverty of the pre-war years is nowhere more visible than in the simple facts that the Japanese are not only living longer, but also getting physically bigger. Life expectancy in the mid-1930s stood at 47 years for men and 50 for women; by the mid 1970s the figures were 72 and 77 respectively. Over the

same period the infant mortality rate fell from 115 per 1,000 to 10. In 1975 the average Japanese male student of 17 was fully 7 centimetres taller than his pre-war counterpart and 5.5 kilogrammes heavier. Improved standards of health reflect not only better medical services but also a more nutritious and protein-rich diet than ever before.

WOMEN

In the words of a saying of the time, "after the war two things became stronger — women and nylon stockings". The new constitution (see page 54) gave women equal rights with men in politics, law and education. But Japanese attitudes towards the position of women in society have changed only slowly. Women are better educated than ever before, but there are

44 Average life expectancy in Japan is now the highest in the world. But can the rapidly rising number of pensioners be provided with adequate incomes, homes and medical care?

still very few female university professors. Women are more conscientious in voting than men, but there are few women politicians. And, although a wider range of careers than ever is open to women, and an increasing proportion of married women are in full-time employment, it is still true that women are significantly worse off than men in almost any kind of employment when it comes to pay, job security or promotion prospects.

There is a "women's movement" in Japan, and the tide of change is undoubtedly flowing in its direction; but "*oomanzu-ribbu*" (women's lib) has little appeal for most Japanese females. Although more of them want to work, at least part-time, the ideal of the majority still centres on a home and family. The Japanese marriage

75

is perhaps more of a genuine partnership than it was in the past, but there is still, in most homes, a clear division of labour. The man's responsibility is to work and provide the family income; the woman's is to care for the home and bring up the children. The role of mother tends to take precedence, both in terms of time and emotional intensity, over the role of wife. Few Japanese couples spend their leisure time outside the home together *as couples*; a man will tend to go drinking or bowling with his work-mates, while his wife chats with neighbours or relatives or involves herself in community organizations or a parent-teacher association.

To the foreign observer, Japanese men still seem to be very much the dominant sex, waited upon by gentle, graceful women both in the office and the home. But appearances are deceptive. A Japanese wife never contradicts her husband — *in public*. In 90 per cent of Japanese homes it is the wife, not the husband,

45 Relaxing with the ancestors. Families enjoy a graveside picnic at the time of the autumn equinox, when the sun sets in the true West, showing where the Buddha is to be found.

who manages the family finances. It is invariably the wife who takes the initiative in major decisions about family holidays or the education of the children, although father may seem to have the final say. It is perhaps significant that the divorce rate is lower in Japan than in the West (about half the British level) and that the rate of remarriage by widows and divorcees is much lower still (about 5 per cent compared with more than 60 per cent in the USA). This suggests that Japanese wives know how to live with Japanese husbands, but have little wish to experience the relationship more than once. As a Japanese proverb neatly puts it, "a husband should be two things, healthy and at work".

RELIGION

Travel posters give an impression of Japan as a "land of festivals", a country of shrines and temples. In the sense that elaborate religious ceremonies are still performed each year and that holy places attract tens of millions of Japanese visitors, this impression is a true one. But Japanese society cannot be said to be dominated by religion in the way that India is dominated by Hinduism or Saudi Arabia by Islam. Japanese spend little of their time or money on religious activities. Religious leaders and organizations exert little influence in public life. Most Japanese deny that religion has any great part to play in their daily lives; but most will, nevertheless, visit a temple at New Year and clean the family grave at the mid-summer festival of O-Bon.

Births, marriages and deaths are still marked by religious ceremonies; and many self-styled non-believers will resort to prayers and offerings to express gratitude for good fortune or to help them cope with a personal crisis.

Post-war Japan has also seen the emergence and flourishing of a number of so-called "New Religions", most of which combine traditional Buddhist or Shinto beliefs and rituals with Western doctrines and forms of church organization. (Christianity as such has made little headway and there are still less than a million Christians of all denominations in the whole country.) Followers of the "New Religions" number significant proportions of the old and

46 A book shop. Reading is a favourite pastime in Japan and the rate of literacy is among the highest in the world.

47 Hibiya, the theatre and film district of Tokyo. American influence is clearly evident in the mass media.

EDUCATION

the less successful. The most significant single movement is the *Soka Gakkai* (Value-Creating Society), a Buddhist sect which claims more than 15 million members, runs its own newspapers, university and symphony orchestra and even established a major political party, the *Komeito* (Clean Government Party).

Japan's biggest industry is education. Like other Japanese industries, it is competitive and efficient and demands total commitment. Schooling is compulsory in Japan from the ages of 6 to 15; but since post-war reforms made access to education open to all, fewer and fewer Japanese have

Changes in post-war society

	1960	1970	1975	1978
Membership of trade unions (000)	7,516	11,481	12,473	n.a.
Monthly income of average workers' household (000 yen)	6.51	112.9	236.2	304.6
Average daily protein intake (grms)	70	78	80	80
Average daily fish intake (grms)	77	87	94	93
Average daily meat intake (grms)	19	43	64	69
Average daily milk intake (grms)	30	68	98	103
Newspaper circulation (000)	37,039	53,023	58,580	63,732
TV owners (000)	6,860	22,819	26,545	28,394
Cinemas	7,457	3,246	2,443	2,392

been content to see their children's schooling limited to 9 years. More than half of pre-school children are in nursery or kindergarten. More than 90 per cent of teenagers stay on to complete senior high school (16-18 years), and nearly 40 per cent of those go on to one of the country's four hundred odd universities and colleges. By entering a top university such as Tokyo or Waseda, a student can virtually guarantee himself secure and well-paid employment for life. Major government departments and leading companies only recruit from the elite universities. School life is therefore geared to the race for university entrance, and the result is what the Japanese themselves call "examination hell". Critics of the system, which produces hundreds of school-age suicides each year, must concede, however, that Japan, despite its formidably difficult writing system, has virtually no illiteracy and employers can assume a level of numeracy and scientific awareness among ordinary workers which is probably unparalleled in the industrial world.

The Japanese are a people hungry for information. Newspaper readership levels are among the highest in the world. Practically every household subscribes to two daily papers, each with a morning and evening edition. And newspapers expect their readers to want news rather than cartoons, pictures and gossip. The large volume of book sales (more than 30,000 new titles are published each year) likewise testifies to the high level of general culture. The nation's numerous television channels (7 in the Tokyo area) do broadcast a great deal of "light entertainment" in the form of cartoon films, quiz shows and "family dramas", but news and current affairs programmes and serious documentaries also attract large viewing audiences. The Japanese are intensely curious about the rest of the world, which for most of them really is "the outside world". The country's well-developed mass media therefore play a major role in informing public opinion as well as providing entertainment.

LEISURE ACTIVITIES

It is perhaps in the related fields of sport, leisure and the arts that the coexistence of tradition and modernity in the Japanese way of life can most clearly be seen. Although the "martial arts" (judo, aikido, kendo, etc) fell into disfavour in the immediate post-war period, interest in them has been greatly revived in recent years. The tea ceremony, calligraphy and flower-arranging have never lost their popularity and are now becoming more widely appreciated in Western countries, as Western music and drama have long been accepted in Japan. In terms of participation, the most popular sport is volleyball; in terms of spectators, baseball (which has been played in Japan for more than a century) and sumo, a traditional style of wrestling. Affluence has made it possible for the Japanese to engage in a wider range of leisure pursuits than ever before, but there is no sign that this is at the expense of those which are most distinctively Japanese.

79

Tradition lives — 48 the festival of Shichi-go-san (15 November) when children aged 7, 5 and 3 are taken to a shrine to thank the gods for their health and growth; 49 carp streamers fly on Boys' Day, one for each boy in the family; 50 kabuki, the most popular of the traditional forms of drama; 51 the Japanese sense of beauty is applied to everyday matters, such as the presentation of food.

YOUNG HISTORIAN

A

1 What evidence can you find that Japan is an affluent society?

2 Why has education become so important in post-war Japan? In what senses is it an industry?

3 Explain what is meant by (a) kimono, (b) "salaryman", (c) hierarchy, (d) paternalistic, (e) consumer durables, (f) calligraphy.

B

1 Write a conversation between a young Japanese housewife and her grandmother, covering such topics as child-care, housework, leisure and family life.

2 Find out how the Japanese system of education differs from that of your own country. In what ways are they similar?

C

1 Which aspects of Japanese society seem to you to be most "traditional"? Which aspects of your own society are "traditional"?

2 Are there any ways in which you think the Japanese are worse off than they were before the war?

D

Draw up a balance sheet, contrasting the most important changes which distinguish the Japan of today from the Japan of the 1930s.

THE SILENT SUPERPOWER

JAPAN AND THE UNITED STATES

Since 1945 Japan's alliance with the United States has been the cornerstone of its foreign policy, but the relationship has passed through several distinct phases, each marked by an increasing movement towards greater independence of action by Japan.

(a) the occupation period. Until the signature of the San Francisco peace treaty on 8 September 1951 (which came into force 28 April 1952), Japan did not enjoy full sovereignty and its foreign relations were effectively controlled by the USA.

(b) from 1951 until the revision of the Security Treaty in 1960. Japan largely accepted American leadership in world politics and took few initiatives of its own.

(c) from 1960 to 1971. A less one-sided relationship began to develop as the last outstanding problems of the war were cleared up, Japan's economic recovery boosted the country's self-confidence, and the "Nixon shocks" of 1971 warned Japan against over-reliance on the "American connection".

(d) since 1971. While the US alliance remained the basis of Japan's defence strategy, in other matters Japan strove increasingly to develop its own policies and priorities.

The San Francisco treaty represented a "majority peace", as the Soviet Union and its Communist allies were not among the signatories. Within hours of its conclusion Prime Minister Yoshida signed a Japan-US Security Treaty which bound Japan to supply bases for the US and recognized the right of US occupation forces (at that time numbering 260,000 in 2,824 bases) to remain on Japanese soil and provided for their possible intervention in case of internal disorder in Japan. No date was set for the ending of the treaty.

Yoshida's critics called for an "overall peace" and pointed out that, by binding Japan to the United States, he was committing the country to support for Chiang Kai-Shek's Nationalist regime in Taiwan, rather than for Mao Tse-tung's Communist "People's Republic" which controlled the whole mainland of China. In addition to this, the US-Russian hostility of the "Cold War" period necessarily complicated Japan's relations with the USSR. Yoshida insisted that he had taken the best course realistically open to him.

The terms of the revised Security Treaty of 1960 showed a much more equal relationship between the two powers:

— Japan was recognized as an equal partner in the preservation of peace in the Far East. Armed attack on *either* partner was to be regarded as a common danger. Consultation was provided for, whenever Japanese security or regional stability were threatened or when American forces on Japanese territories were moved.

— A ten-year term was set for the pact, with termination subject to one year's notice. (It was renewed in 1970.)

— No nuclear weapons were to be located in Japan without Japanese consent.

— Japan was relieved of contributions toward the payment of American troops.

— The provision for US intervention in the

event of large-scale Japanese riots was dropped.

Although these terms considerably enhanced Japan's status in the alliance, widespread opposition to the acceptance of the revised treaty developed rapidly. Many Japanese, especially on the left wing, objected because it compromised Japan's relations with China and Russia, and others, because it seemed to point the way to the possibility of Japanese re-armament. The Socialist Party therefore took the lead in blocking discussion of the treaty in the Diet. But Prime Minister Kishi was not to be deterred. The LDP had a clear majority in the Diet and when the Socialists rejected a proposal for a 50-day extension of the parliamentary session to allow for further discussion of the treaty, Kishi used his majority to force a vote approving the extension. This perfectly legal action was thought by many — even inside the LDP — to be very "un-Japanese" and quite contrary to the proper course of action which would obligate a national leader to seek harmonious consensus on fundamental issues. Enraged Socialist deputies boycotted parliamentary sessions, and daily street demonstrations, involving hundreds of thousands of protestors, were orchestrated by trade unions and student organizations.

Kishi nevertheless pressed forward with the ratification of the treaty. When he resigned immediately afterwards, the mass agitation quickly died away. He was perhaps right in saying that he would be guided by the "mute voice" of the majority rather than by the slogans of the chanting mobs which swirled around the Diet building.

The resolution of other outstanding issues in the field of US-Japanese relations provoked less dramatic concern.

— In 1960 the United States paroled the last hundred Japanese war criminals, held in prison in Tokyo.

— In 1962 agreement was finally reached over Japan's contribution to the costs of the occupation — $490 million (a quarter of the estimated total) to be repaid over 15 years, most of it to go to developing countries with which both the US and Japan wished to strengthen relations.

— In 1968 the Bonin Islands and Iwo Jima were returned to Japanese control. Okinawa, with a population of one million, proved to be more problematic. The US had invested over $1,000 million in military installations on the island, which it regarded as a key base for operations in East Asia. But the local population, and Japanese opinion generally, was hostile to continued American control. The US finally renounced all rights and interests in the island in 1972, but was permitted to continue use of its military facilities.

As military and territorial issues were gradually resolved, economic and diplomatic differences began to assume greater importance in Japan-US relations. American manufacturers consistently complained of unfair competition from Japanese rivals, and in 1961 a Joint United States-Japan Committee on Trade and Economic Affairs was set up, to iron out mutual difficulties in a series of annual meetings. Despite the closeness of the contacts which developed through these and other exchanges, relations between the two powers could still be clouded by uncertainties and misunderstandings, as the events of 1971 were to show.

In July 1971 President Nixon suddenly announced that he would shortly visit Peking, a dramatic prelude to the restoration of full diplomatic relations between the USA and the People's Republic of China and thus a fundamental re-orientation of America's entire post-war policy towards Communist China. Tokyo diplomats were as greatly astounded as any in the world, having been given no prior warning of this major initiative on the part of their chief ally. A month later the US government made another sudden announcement — it was introducing a package of economic measures designed to improve the American balance of payments, including the floating of the dollar in terms of gold and a 10 per cent surcharge on imports entering the USA. As Japan sent about 30 per cent of its exports to the USA, it could not but regard this as a major blow.

From isolation to expanding international relations — 52 the island of Dejima in Nagasaki Harbour, on which Dutch traders were confined during the Tokugawa period; 53 the Japanese ambassador to Spain inaugurates a new Japan Air Lines service (Madrid-Tokyo), 1980. Increasing numbers of Japanese have the opportunity to travel abroad.

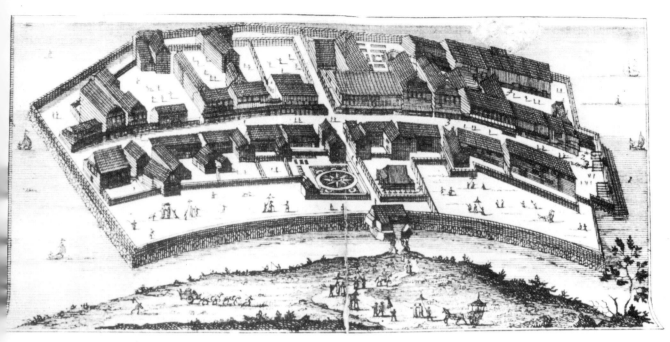

54 The cornerstone — prime minister Fukuda signs another agreement with the United States, Japan's chief ally and customer.

In practice, these "Nixon shocks", as the Japanese called them, presented Japan with no insurmountable problems. The Tanaka government followed America's lead in normalizing relations with China (see page 89). And, as the Americans had intended, the import surcharges were modified in return for an upward revaluation of the yen, which made Japanese goods dearer in the American market. What mattered to the Japanese was the abrupt way in which these changes had been forced on them. Diplomats and businessmen alike feared that Japan had come to rely too heavily on American goodwill and protection and, further, that this reliance might prove, in the light of the "Nixon shocks" and America's withdrawal from Vietnam, to be quite unjustified. Japan had relied for a quarter of a century on the American "nuclear umbrella" for its defence. Could it continue to do so?

Japanese disarmament, pursued so thoroughly in the early days of the occupation, had been halted and reversed with the accession to power of the Communists in China. Beginning with the establishment in 1950 of a lightly-armed "National Police Reserve", the Japanese authorities, with American assistance and increasingly under American pressure, started to build up a "Self-Defence Force" (SDF) comprising land, air and maritime units. The constitutionality of these forces (in terms of Article IX of the 1946 Constitution) has been challenged by various left-wing groups and individuals, but the challenge has not been upheld by the courts and the SDF has gradually won the grudging acceptance of a public which has not yet forgotten the disastrous influence of the military on Japanese life in the pre-war period.

During the 1970s, as successive American governments experienced economic difficulties at home and diplomatic defeats abroad, the idea that Japan should play a larger part in "sharing the burden" of its defence came to look increasingly attractive to many American politicians and taxpayers. Japan's response was to continue the modernization of its military equipment and to improve conditions of service for SDF personnel. But a wholesale enlargement of Japan's armed establishment was resolutely resisted, for the following reasons:

(a) Japanese public opinion would oppose any significant strengthening of the military beyond the level necessary for it to perform its basic tasks — which were to oppose any aggressor while America mobilized its main forces (usually estimated to take three days) and to perform rescue and relief duties in cases of natural disaster.

(b) Increased defence spending would mean increased taxes.

(c) Only if Japan's military forces were massively enlarged would a significant shift in the strategic balance in North-East Asia be achieved; but such a move would necessarily alarm and possibly antagonize Japan's neighbours and trading partners in East and South-East Asia. By heightening tension in the region, re-armament would jeopardize rather than strengthen Japan's security.

Suggestions that Japan should develop a nuclear armoury have been decisively rejected by successive governments pledged to the "three principles" that Japan should neither produce, possess nor introduce such weapons on Japanese soil. Japan has considerable expertise in the fields of rocketry and nuclear power generation, but the general public remains, for obvious reasons, strongly opposed to nuclear weapons.

Japanese opponents of further re-armament also point out that Japan does make a contribution to the stability of East and South-East Asia by promoting economic development in those areas and by providing the US with base facilities. Whether the United States will continue to press Japan to play a larger military role and with what success, only the future can tell.

55   Something to teach — Japan's foreign aid is growing rapidly and Japan can offer expert training in the skills of fishing and rice-growing.

JAPAN AND THE SOVIET UNION

Japan's post-war relations with the Soviet Union have been, to say the least, rather distant. Diplomatic relations between the two states were not established until 1956 and there is still no formal peace treaty between them. The major outstanding point of dispute is the continued Soviet occupation of four islands of the southern Kurile chain, seized in the closing days of the war. Japan regards these "Northern Territories" as an integral part of its homeland and refuses to renounce its claim to sovereignty over them. Disputes over fishing grounds and the general build-up of Soviet naval strength in the Western Pacific also serve to maintain tension between the two states. On the other hand, Russia's

eagerness to take advantage of Japan's technological know-how, coupled with Japan's appetite for Russia's resources, point to the possibilities of fruitful co-operation in the economic development of Eastern Siberia. However, progress in this area rests, in part, on not antagonizing the Chinese, who remain deeply suspicious of alleged Russian desires for "hegemonism" (i.e. regional dominance).

56 On alert — Japan's Self Defence Forces must provide the nation's first line of protection against possible foreign aggression.

JAPAN AND CHINA

Japanese attitudes toward China have, since 1949, been a strained mixture of attraction and repulsion. Left-wingers have admired the People's Republic as a model of the revolutionary society and as the most outspoken critic of the United States. Right-wingers have acknowledged Japan's great cultural debt to the heritage of Chinese civilization and have dreamed of the massive economic opportunities offered by China's wealth of natural resources and, since the accession to power of Teng Hsiao-Ping, the Chinese hunger for advanced technology. On the other hand, most ordinary Japanese have no great regard for the Communist form of society and all Japanese diplomats are acutely sensitive to the many problems created by continuing Sino-Soviet hostility. From Japan's point of view, the difficulty is to develop closer links with Peking without arousing the wrath of Moscow. During the 1950s and 1960s Japan followed America's policy of recognizing the Nationalist regime in Taiwan as the "true" China; but contacts with the People's Republic were maintained by means of trade conducted through "friendly firms" controlled by Japanese trade unions and left-wing political parties. Nixon's reversal of America's China policy was followed by the rapid development of closer links between Tokyo and Peking, culminating in a "Treaty of Peace and Friendship" signed in August 1978. This ten-year pact pledges both states to abstain from the use of force. At the insistence of the Chinese, the treaty contains a clause opposing "hegemonism" in East Asia. Japan accepted this with some reluctance, in the face of strenuous protests from Russia.

JAPAN AND THE KOREAN PENINSULA

The nearest point on the Asian mainland to Japan is the Korean peninsula, divided since the

1952 cease-fire at the 38th parallel between capitalist South Korea and Communist North Korea. Both states are highly armed and the air forces of either could reach Japanese territory within fifteen minutes' flying time. Japanese relations with the peninsula are further complicated by the memory of Japan's harsh colonial rule there in the period 1910-45 and by the fact that Japan's own Korean minority is divided in its allegiance between North and South. Japan does not recognize the North Korean regime and Japanese business has invested heavily in the rapidly industrializing economy of the South. Fearful, above all, of the forceful reunification of the peninsula by a North Korean invasion, Japan remains anxious that the United States should continue to guarantee the security of South Korea by maintaining at least token forces in the area.

JAPAN AND SOUTH-EAST ASIA

The states of South-East Asia are of the utmost economic importance to Japan, both as markets for its manufactures and as a source of raw materials, energy and food-stuffs. Also, the Middle Eastern oil which supplies most of Japan's fuel needs must pass through this region. A South-East Asian country hostile to Japan could threaten to strangle Japanese industry by intercepting oil supplies. Japan therefore has the most powerful practical reasons for wishing to cultivate good relations with the ASEAN countries (Association of South East Asian Nations — Malaysia, Singapore, Thailand, Philippines, Indonesia). But again, this task has been complicated by bitter memories of wartime occupation and by resentment of the power of Japan's great manufacturing corporations. This resentment exploded in a series of student demonstrations during a South-East Asian tour made by prime minister Tanaka in 1974. The major accusations made against the Japanese were that they were stripping the region of its raw materials, failing to plough back their profits into the local economies and making no effort to train local employees to assume posts of higher responsibility. These

criticisms prompted much debate in Japan and led to promises that Japanese business practices would be revised and that Japanese aid to the region would be doubled within three years. When prime minister Fukuda toured the region again in 1977 his reception was courteous and cordial. In a speech at Manila the Japanese leader set out the "Fukuda doctrine" which would henceforth guide Japan's policies in the region:

> Japan . . . rejects the role of a military power and . . . is resolved to contribute to the peace and prosperity of South-East Asia and . . . will do its best to consolidate the relationship of mutual confidence . . . with these countries, in wide-ranging fields covering not only political and economic areas but also social and cultural areas.

However, Japan is so much more powerful economically and advanced technologically than the ASEAN states that it must be cautious in taking initiatives lest it arouse fears that its ultimate aim is not to assist but to dominate.

JAPAN AND THE REST OF THE WORLD

The growth of Japan's economy has increased Japanese dependence on ever-more distant markets and sources of supply, a dependence forcefully emphasized by the "shock" of the 1973 oil price rise. Japan's prosperity and stability depends, therefore, not merely on good relations with the superpowers and its immediate neighbours, but also on its links with the EEC, Australasia, the Gulf States, Africa and Latin America. An economic superpower but a military mini-power, Japan, as a disarmed democracy committed to interdependence with others, has an important role to play in international affairs. But, for all its acknowledged power, Japan is still troubled by a sense of uncertainty. In many ways ideally suited to mediate between Western and non-Western countries, Japan seems to hesitate in taking a lead, to wait for a cue from others. Consider the general remarks of prime minister Ohira, questioned about the

歓イギリス教員グループ様迎

broad questions of Japan's world role on the eve of the Tokyo summit in 1979:

> . . . we consider it of utmost importance to be a member in good standing in the global community. In other words, in our domestic and foreign policies, we must conduct ourselves in a way the rest of the world can understand and approve of. At the very least, we must act in such a way so as not to fall out of step with the standards of conduct that govern the world at large.

A generation after Hiroshima, Japan remains an uncertain state in an uncertain world.

57 Getting to know you — Japanese officials pose with a visiting group of British teachers. The Japanese are concerned that foreigners know little about their country and way of life.

91

YOUNG HISTORIAN

A

1 Why has Japan been so closely allied to the United States since 1945? Why is this link likely to remain a close one?

2 Why has Japan not enjoyed good relations with the Soviet Union?

3 Why are China, Korea and the South-East Asian nations especially important to Japan?

4 Of what importance to Japan are Africa, Latin America, the Middle East and the EEC?

5 Explain the meaning of (a) consultation, (b) consensus, (c) ratification, (d) surcharge, (e) normalizing, (f) revaluation, (g) hegemonism.

B

1 Discuss the case for and against total Japanese disarmament.

2 What has Japan got to offer the developing countries? Find out about Japan's overseas aid programme.

C

Write a series of headlines covering the most important turning-points in Japan's post-war foreign relations.

D

Design a poster to encourage foreign students to come to study in Japan. Why should Japan wish to encourage this?

DATE LIST

1853	Arrival of Commodore Perry
1868	End of Tokugawa rule
1868	Edo, re-named Tokyo, becomes national capital
1871	Introduction of modern postal system, currency and local government
1872	Establishment of first primary schools, railway, banks and spinning mill
1889	Meiji Constitution
1894-95	Sino-Japanese war
1902	Anglo-Japanese alliance
1904-5	Russo-Japanese war
1910	Japan annexes Korea
1912	Death of emperor Meiji
1918	Rice riots and Siberian expedition
1920	Japan joins League of Nations
1922	Washington Naval Treaty
1923	Tokyo and Yokohama severely damaged by earthquake
1925	Adult males given the vote
1926	Hirohito succeeds Taisho as emperor
1930	Japan signs London Naval Treaty. Hamaguchi shot
1931	Manchurian Incident
1932	Establishment of Manchukuo
1933	Japan leaves League of Nations
1937	Japanese attempt conquest of China
1940	Japan allies with Germany and Italy
1941	Japan goes to war with the US and Britain
1945	Atom bombs dropped on Hiroshima and Nagasaki. Japan surrenders
1946	Showa Constitution establishes democracy
1949	Dr Hideki Yukawa wins Nobel Prize for Physics
1952	End of Allied occupation
1953	TV broadcasting begins in Japan
1956	Japan joins the United Nations
1960	Revision of Japan-US Mutual Security Treaty causes riots
1964	18th Olympic Games held in Tokyo. "Bullet-train" service begins
1968	Yasunari Kawabata wins Nobel Prize for Literature
1970	Expo' 70 International exhibition held at Osaka
1972	Winter Olympics held at Sapporo
1972	Okinawa returned to Japan
1973	Oil price rise hits Japanese economy
1974	Former prime minister Eisaku Sato wins Nobel Prize for Peace

BOOKS FOR FURTHER READING

Pat Barr, *Foreign Devils* (Penguin)

W.G. Beasley, *The Modern History of Japan* (Weidenfeld & Nicholson, 1973)

H. Bolitho, *Meiji Japan* (Cambridge University Press, 1977)

C.J. Dunn, *Everyday Life in Traditional Japan* (Batsford)

M. Gibson, *The Rise of Japan* (Wayland, 1972)

Ian Nish, *The Story of Japan* (Faber, 1968)

Paul Norbury, *Introducing Japan* (Paul Norbury Publications, 1977)

E. O'Connor, *Japan's Modernization* (Harrap, 1975)

E. O'Connor, *The Wealth of Japan* (Harrap,1976)

R. Parkinson, *Attack on Pearl Harbour* (Wayland, 1973)

E.O. Reischauer, *Japan: Past & Present* (Duckworth, 1970)

R. Sims, *Modern Japan* (Bodley Head)

Richard Storry, *A History of Modern Japan* (Penguin, 1969)

Richard Tames, *Japan Today* (Kaye & Ward, 1976)

Richard Tames, *The Japan Handbook*, 2nd edition (Paul Norbury Publications)

B. Williams, *Modern Japan* (Longman, 1969)

N. Zepke, *The Hundred Year Miracle* (Heinemann, 1977)

INDEX

The numbers in **bold type** refer to figure numbers of the illustrations

Adams, William 5, 10
agriculture 25, 51, 64, 72; **3, 41**
Anglo-Japanese Alliance 17, 23
armed forces 15, 25, 37-9, 54, 86-7, 90; **12, 13, 16, 21, 26, 56**
atomic bomb 42-6
Australia 22, 29

Benedict, Ruth 39
Boxer Rising 17
Buddhism 3, 11, 77-8; **45**

China 3, 4, 11, 16, 18, 21-4, 27, 31-2, 42, 50, 86, 89; **21, 22**
Christianity 3, 11, 77
Churchill 37, 43
"closed country" 11; **52**
Cold War 53, 83
Communists 25, 51, 60
Constitution:
  Meiji 15
  Showa 49, 51, 54-8, 75, 86
Co-Prosperity Sphere 34, 38-9
Coral Sea, Battle of the 39

democracy 3, 9, 15, 21, 25, 48-9, 53, 54-63; **14, 33, 34, 36, 37, 38**
Diet, National 15, 21, 55-7; **33, 34**
Dutch 11; **52**

economic miracle 66-70; **39, 41, 42, 43**
education 14-15, 50-1, 67, 78-9
energy 3, 64, 73
extra-territoriality 12, 17, 24

First World War 21-2, 25
foreign experts 14-15
Fuji, Mount **1**

genro 25

Hamaguchi 27
Hirohito 26, 43, 49, 50, 54; **18, 31, 33**

Hiroshima 43, 69, 91
Hokkaido 14, 51

Ikeda 64
industry 14, 15, 21, 25, 52, 64-70, 73; **42**

Japanese 3, 4, 17, 42, 44, 45, 46
  foreign views of 4-6; **57**
  generalizations about 3, 6, 9, 10, 39
  knowledge of 3
  language of 3, 4, 74
  overseas 3; **15, 19, 53, 55**

Kamikaze 41-2
Kipling, Rudyard 4
Kishi 84
Korea 14, 16-18, 29, 53, 64, 69, 89-90
Koreans 3, 39

League of Nations 22, 31
leisure 79; **44, 47, 50**
Liberal-Democratic Party 59-60, 67, 84
literacy 14, 49; **46**
London Naval Treaty 27

MacArthur, General Douglas 39, 43, 47, 49; **29**
Manchukuo 29-32; **19, 20**
Meiji period 10, 13-20
Meiji restoration 13
Midway, Battle of 39
military influence 4-5, 12, 29-32, 42-3, 48-50; **17**
Mitsui 32, 51
Morris, John 10, 41

Nagasaki 11, 43, 69
Nine Power Treaty 23, 32

occupation 41, 42, 47-53, 54-9, 84; **29, 30**

oil 34, 69, 90
Okinawa 16, 42, 84

Paris Peace Conference 22
Parliament, *see* Diet
Pearl Harbor 34, 36, 40; **24**
Perry, Commodore Matthew 11; **9**
pollution 61-2, 69; **39, 40, 43**
population 3, 25, 29, 70, 74-5
Portsmouth, Treaty of 18
Portuguese 7
prisoners of war 39
purges 50
Pu Yi 31; **18**

religion 6, 45, 48
rice 10, 25; **3, 41**
Roosevelt, Franklin D. 36, 42
Russo-Japanese war 17-18, 39; **11, 12, 13**

Sakhalin 18, 23, 43
Second World War 10, 32-46; **23, 24, 25, 26, 27, 28**
Security Treaty 59, 83
Shidehara 27
Shimonoseki, Treaty of 16
Shinto 3, 32, 55, 77
Showa restoration 26
Siberian intervention 22-3
silk 14, 28
Singapore 23, 36, 90
Sino-Japanese war 16-17
Socialist Party 59-60, 84
Soka Gakkai 60, 78
South-East Asia 10, 34, 36, 64, 87, 90
statistics 4, 50, 64, 72-3, 74

Taisho 21
tariffs 11, 28, 67
television 3, 72, 74, 79; **38**
Tokugawa 10, 11, 12, 14
Tokugawa Ieyasu **8**
Tokyo 14, 32, 41, 64, 74, 79; **5,**

34, 39, 47
trade unions 51-2, 61, 66-7, 79; **14**
tradition **2, 48, 49, 50, 51**
Triple Intervention 16-17; **10**
Truman, Harry S. 42, 43, 46
Twenty-One Demands 21-2

unequal treaties 11-13, 17

United States 11, 15, 18, 22, 27, 28, 34, 36, 39-43, 47-53, 54, 57, 59, 64, 83-7; **9, 24, 29, 47, 54**
USSR 22-3, 43, 49, 53, 88-9

war crimes 42, 49, 50, 84
Washington conference 23-4

women 3, 55, 67, 72, 75-6; **2, 14, 17, 32, 42**

Xavier, St Francis 5

Yoshida, Shigeru 59, 83

zaibatsu 51-3, 64